More ✱ 10-Minute Plays for Teens

THE APPLAUSE ACTING SERIES

More ✳10-Minute Plays for Teens

Edited by
Lawrence Harbison

APPLAUSE
THEATRE & CINEMA BOOKS
An Imprint of Hal Leonard Corporation

Published in 2015 by Applause Theatre & Cinema Books
An Imprint of Hal Leonard Corporation
7777 West Bluemound Road
Milwaukee, WI 53213

Trade Book Division Editorial Offices
33 Plymouth St., Montclair, NJ 07042

Printed in the United States of America

Book design by John J. Flannery

Library of Congress Cataloging-in-Publication Data

Names: Harbison, Lawrence, editor.
Title: More 10-minute plays for teens / edited by Lawrence Harbison.
Description: Milwaukee, WI : Applause Imprint, 2015.
Identifiers: LCCN 2015039379 | ISBN 9781495011801 (pbk.)
Subjects: LCSH: One-act plays, American. | Teenagers--Drama.
Classification: LCC PS627.O53 M67 2015 | DDC 812/.04108--dc23
LC record available at http://lccn.loc.gov/2015039379

www.applausebooks.com

CONTENTS

INTRODUCTION

This anthology contains twelve terrific new plays, all with characters that are teens. All of the plays are easy to produce, and none requires a teen to spray paint his hair gray and pretend to be a geezer. All have subject matter appropriate for production in schools that will, I believe, interest young performers without offending administrators, teachers, or parents. They are written in a wide variety of styles: some are comic (laughs), some are dramatic (no laughs), some are realistic, several are not.

Ten-minute plays are being done as bills all over the world—so why not in schools, too? This volume amounts to one-stop shopping. If you're a teacher who wants to work on short plays in class, or a young actor who wants do a play or plays with your friends, look no further.

There are wonderful plays here by some of the finest practitioners of the ten-minute play form—playwrights such as Don Nigro, Sherry Kramer, and Kayla Cagan, and by others less well known but equally terrific such as Wayne Paul Mattingly, Lesley Anne Moreau, Elayne Heilveil, and Barry Ernst. On the title page of each play you will find information as to how you can procure permission to produce it—which is, after all, the point.

Break a leg!

Lawrence Harbison

More ✳10-Minute Plays for Teens

Edited by
Lawrence Harbison

BEAT UP SUMMER

Barry Ernst

CHARACTERS
ANDY: *age 12*
DANNY: *age 9*
JACK: *age 11*

TIME
The present day.

SETTING
It is 1960, inside an old, abandoned hotel in what is now a residential neighborhood in a small New England town. The hotel has been boarded up and closed for twenty-three years. It is dark inside until we hear voices and see a small light (a flashlight). Three boys run in—two with bikes, very tired and scared, breathing hard . . .

ANDY: [*To* DANNY.] Where's your bike?

DANNY: I left it outside.

ANDY: Go get it! If they see it, they'll know we're here. You want to get us killed?

DANNY: I didn't know. I'm scared!

ANDY: [*To* JACK.] Go get it for him! And hurry up! Stay low and get that bike. And don't get caught. He must have left it out in plain view. [*To* DANNY.] You little [*Pause.*] . . . pip-squeak!

DANNY: It's not my fault. So don't start calling names.

ANDY: [*To* JACK.] Hurry up or I'll kick your butt, too! [JACK *runs out, but stops and carefully looks before he leaves.*]

DANNY: You started it! Why did you say that about his mother!

ANDY: It was about his sister, and it's true!

[JACK *runs back in, with bike, almost out of breath.*]

JACK: [*To* ANDY.] . . . Okay. I brought it in. No one saw me. I looked, but didn't see them. They probably think we're somewhere else. But don't worry, they're out there looking for us and want to get us, bad. That's for sure!

ANDY: They'll never find us here. They think we're too scared to go inside. It's the last place they would look. They know if the neighbors find out they'll call the cops. Even they're too afraid to go inside here. Just be quiet and they'll get tired of looking for us and go away.

DANNY: Do you think they'll catch us?

ANDY: They're too slow and too dumb.

DANNY: What would they do if they caught us?

ANDY: Don't you follow the news? They found three little boys with their throats cut last week somewhere in California. A small town like ours. In the woods by a river.

DANNY: Who did it?

ANDY: They don't know. But they think it was a grown-up. A killer. A man who liked to kill kids. But it might have been other kids. They always blame everything on adults.

JACK: What do we do if they corner us or we don't see them.

ANDY: That's why we have to be careful. Those three kids who got murdered weren't. This is what probably happened. They had their bikes and just went down the wrong street. And those older kids were waiting for them. And when they saw them, they blocked them off so they couldn't get by. And then took out their knives and went towards them. Slowly they crept, step by step. And when the little kids tried to run away, there was no place to go. And they caught them and then took them into the woods. And said to them: "You want to call us names and like to make fun of us? And throw things like crap at us?! And use bad language and think it's funny? And call our mothers bad names? Did you really think we'd never catch you?!"

DANNY: That's what we do. Now I'm really scared.

ANDY: Then the biggest kid smiled and went over to the smallest boy and put his knife to his throat. The other kids thought he was just trying to scare them. But he was really mad. And took the knife. And then cut the kid's throat! And then they probably said something like this: "You killed him! What do we do with him, now?!" So he smiled and went over to the other little kids and killed them, too. Sliced their throats just like that! [*Shows a slicing motion with his hands.*] It took only a second to kill them. And then he said to the other big kids: "And if you ever tell anyone about this, I'll come and get you, too!" And so all of them got on their bikes and got out of there as fast as they could go.

DANNY: How do you know all of this?!

ANDY: I made it up, but that's probably what could have happened.

DANNY: What would we do if some little kids threw dog crap and bees at us and called our parents terrible names like we do to them? Would we kill them?

ANDY: I wouldn't kill them, but I'd definitely kick their butts so they wouldn't ever do it again. But I think they are so mad at us, they would do anything to find us. And if they did find us, they won't be able to control their tempers—that's how pissed off they are at us.

DANNY: Maybe we should stop, then. And apologize.

ANDY: It's too late for that, now. They wouldn't accept even if we begged their forgiveness. But I don't want to, anyways. This isn't going to be a beat-up summer, because we're not going to get caught. This is going to be our best summer ever.

JACK: Let's just stop.

ANDY: So what do we do then? Just play Clue and Setback all summer?

DANNY: It's fun.

ANDY: But it's boring. Look at what we're doing now.

JACK: Did you ever know a kid who died? Remember two summers ago when we played wiffle ball at the school every night. I had a good year and tied for second place in home runs. That was my best summer. There was one kid on my team who I didn't know too well. But we were kind of friends. But he didn't play with us last summer because he went to Germany to see his grandparents. I heard that he was riding his bike and some car hit him and he died. I still feel bad about it.

DANNY: My best summer was when I was only five. My parents had taken us to the museum to see the dinosaurs. They were big, with only the bones, but they put them together so you could see what they really looked like millions of years ago. I thought that was so cool. I told my dad I wanted to be a dinosaur scientist, too. And he thought it was a good idea. So all summer long I went into our backyard and dug for dinosaur bones. I thought I was really going to find them in our backyard. I didn't find any, but I sure had a great summer. I almost did though, kind of.

JACK: What do you mean by that? Did you find any?

DANNY: I found chicken bones. I thought at first it might be a baby dinosaur, but my mom told me it probably got in the backyard from our garbage. The bees are exciting, aren't they, Andy.

JACK: Did anyone remember to bring the bees?

DANNY: They are on my bike.

ANDY: Let's see if they're still knocked out. [*To* DANNY.] . . . So go get them! [DANNY *goes over to his bike and takes out a big jar that was in the basket on the handlebars.*] . . . And the strings. They are knocked out so we can tie them. [*Hands strings to* DANNY.] . . . Okay, then so now tie the strings.

DANNY: Why me?

JACK: Don't you want to be tough, you little idiot?

DANNY: What if they wake up?

ANDY: Look—they're out. It's your turn.

DANNY: But I don't know how to tie a knot.

JACK: I'll do the first one. [*Takes jar and opens it and pulls out a knocked-out bee. Then takes a string and ties it to the bee.*] . . . Now you do one. [*Looking very apprehensive,* DANNY *takes a bee out of the jar and tries to tie a string to it but fumbles around and can't seem to get the knot tied . . . then he looks at the bee thinking it might move and jumps, dropping the bee.*]

ANDY: What do you think you're doing, you twerp?

DANNY: It was moving . . .

ANDY: No it wasn't. You're just afraid!

[JACK *goes over and starts tying each bee—doing them very fast until he finishes them.*]

JACK: That wasn't so hard once you get the hang of it. But if you're a scary cat like you are . . .

DANNY: Then what do we do with them now?

ANDY: When we get out of here, we'll go by the country club. They're probably there shagging balls. The bees will be awake by then. And very mad. So when we ride by those jerks, we'll twirl the bees and then toss them at them and then ride fast and get away.

JACK: That will really get them mad. When they're making money. They'll probably all get fired.

[ANDY *and* JACK *both start laughing.*]

DANNY: We really want to sting them?

ANDY: I do.

JACK: When I was nine they made fun of my name. And called me a girl.

DANNY: I got them last year.

ANDY: How was that?

DANNY: Remember that night we played flashlight tag with them last summer? I thought I was going to get caught. But Teddy didn't see me. He put the flashlight in my area, but I laid down flat and tricked him. Then he walked right by me and thought I was a rock and stood on top of me. It really hurt, because he's so big. And he kept stepping down real hard on me. I almost gave myself away laughing. But he didn't know it was me.

ANDY: He knew it was you all along, you dumb little kid. Why do you think he kept pushing on you? To hurt you. He put all his weight on you and pushed down hard, right?

DANNY: Yeah. Do you think he really knew? He never said anything. And I got home free. I thought I tricked him.

JACK: Get real, man. He had his fun crushing you.

DANNY: I still think I tricked him!

[ANDY *starts walking around the floor of the hotel. The others follow him. There are boxes all around with all kinds of things in them: furnishings, pictures, books and ledgers, old newspapers, and so on*].

ANDY: I always wanted to sneak in here. I never thought we'd use it as a hideout. My father told me stories about this place. When he was a kid, they used to go to dinner at the hotel. They would go twice a year, because the hotel had the best and most expensive restaurant in town. He said it made his parents feel important to come here even though they weren't rich. They would dress up in their finest. My grandpa would wear his Sunday suit, Grandma her best dress, and the kids their church clothes. My dad told me this was the most important building in town. But they closed it in 1937, twenty-three years ago. Even before the war.

JACK: They don't want us in here, you know. Just look at all the stuff here.

ANDY: It's really cool.

[ANDY *starts crawling around and the others follow.*]

DANNY: Why are we crawling? Is it a game?

JACK: We're just being careful. We don't know what's inside here or next door. We've never been in a place like this . . . [*Looks at* ANDY.] . . . Right?

ANDY: Just don't talk too loud. If the neighbors hear us, they'll automatically call the cops. My dad calls them nosy parkers. They have nothing better to do with their lives. And they don't like kids.

DANNY: What would they do to us?

JACK: What do you think?!

DANNY: We learn in school that the police are our friends and we can tell them anything.

[JACK *suddenly hits* DANNY *in the stomach.*]

DANNY: [*Angry.*] . . . What was that for?! [*Goes at him.*] . . . He hit me!

ANDY: I told you to shut up. If you don't, you'll get another one—this time harder.

JACK: I'm trying to teach him something, but he doesn't want to learn. You can't trust anyone, especially them. That's what they'll do to us if they catch us. Except a hundred times worse. They don't like it if they told us not to go here and there are signs and we still won't listen. These cops don't want to spend all of their time running after kids like us. They're mad because they have their own kids to deal with who don't listen to them, and they don't like it. So they'll take it out on us if they catch us.

ANDY: [*The boys are still on their hands and knees, crawling like they are hiding from somebody.*] Get up.

[*All three stand up.*]

DANNY: [DANNY *takes a picture out of one of the boxes.*] . . . Look at this.

ANDY: [*Looks at picture.*] . . . It's a family. Parents and their three little girls. Look at all of these old newspapers in the boxes, too. This one is from October 10, 1910. Wow! It's about the flood. We studied about it in school. On the front page of the *Clarion*. Main Street was half under water. There's Davis's Pharmacy, just where it is now, but the water is almost up to the front entrance.

JACK: They had to rebuild part of the town because of the damage from the flood.

DANNY: I wonder who those little girls are. They probably are pretty old now. Maybe that's my grandmother. She has two sisters. I'm going to ask her.

ANDY: Maybe we can find the hidden room.

JACK: What do you mean?

ANDY: There is a hidden room in this hotel where they did gambling and stuff. And a lot of drinking. It used to be against the law, but they still did it.

JACK: We've been through five rooms so far. But no place for gambling.

ANDY: I said it was hidden. We have to find it. It's going to be hard in the dark. Because back then they didn't want anyone to know where it was.

JACK: Even though everyone knew about it?

ANDY: Everyone knew they did gambling here, but they still wanted to hide it. You won't find it mentioned in any of those old newspapers. But it was a secret that everyone knew.

DANNY: [*Points.*] . . . Maybe it's over there!

JACK: All I can see are boxes with pictures and books and old furniture.

DANNY: This is the best adventure we've ever had. I want to find the gambling room. What does it look like?

ANDY: I guess there's tables. With numbers on them. And cards. And maybe even some money.

JACK: Wow . . . What would we do then?

ANDY: If we find it, we keep it!

DANNY: The police would really be mad at us then. Isn't that stealing?

ANDY: I don't think so. If no one else ever found it. And we did. It would be ours. Kind of like buried treasure.

DANNY: Maybe this is my best summer, after all.

JACK: We could spend all week here and still not see every room in the hotel. And probably never find the hidden room.

ANDY: I wonder what the hotel restaurant looks like. In all of these boxes, I wonder if there is an old diagram of the entire hotel.

DANNY: No one knows we're here.

JACK: Or would ever know we were here.

DANNY: What does he mean by that?

ANDY: He means that if we get killed and never came home, they'd never find us.

JACK: And we might not even be the only dead bodies in here.

ANDY: Do you think anyone ever got shot? Maybe that's why they kept the hidden room a secret. Maybe somebody was cheating at gambling and someone got mad and killed him.

JACK: This place is probably full of ghosts.

ANDY: [*To* DANNY.] . . . Maybe we'll be ghosts, too, and never get out of here. We'll haunt this place forever and ever. [*He laughs.*]

> [*The boys hear banging. They jump up. A beat. Then clanking. They fly into each others' arms. Another beat. Things begin falling down. The boys become even more scared, especially* ANDY. *A beat. A strong wind gusts across the stage. A beat. Doors begin to open and close* . . .]

DANNY: [*Very scared.*] . . . What was that?! Let's get out of here!

JACK: [*Scared, too.*] . . . Maybe he's right!

ANDY: [*Very scared.*] . . . I know. I was trying to scare him and I scared myself, too.

JACK: I think there's probably ghosts here.

ANDY: If there are ghosts, then they're here. Right now, looking at us. I know some people died here. [*To* JACK.] . . . Take a look to see if the coast is clear.

[JACK *walks away, looks out, and then returns and nods his head yes.*]

JACK: I don't see anyone. Let's make a break for it now!

DANNY: Then what about the bees?

ANDY: Forget about them!

DANNY: Then there's going to be bee ghosts in here, too.

ANDY: But not us. I don't want to be a ghost.

JACK: But if they catch us, we're as good as dead.

DANNY: At least we won't be in here. With all of the bees and rats and people who got killed in this hotel.

[*There is a cacophony of sounds and noises. All three run as fast as they can toward the doors—*JACK *and* DANNY *grab their bikes fast.* ANDY, *who is running with them, suddenly stops and walks to center stage . . .*]

JACK: What, are you crazy?! What are you doing? Let's get out of here!

[*Lighting is on* ANDY *as he looks at the audience. The other two boys are anxiously standing at the exit door urging him through their motions to go.*]

ANDY: [*To audience.*] We somehow survived that summer without getting killed. There were some close calls. But they never caught us. What we didn't know and what no one knows including me is that many of the secrets and the history of our town was in the hundreds of boxes in dozens of rooms in this hotel. Like the picture of that family. [*Holds up picture.*] In another box on another floor was this newspaper headline from 1920: FAMILY DIES IN MYSTE-RIOUS FIRE. Those were the children, exactly our ages—twelve, eleven, and nine. So no one was ever able to put it all together and everything was destroyed in 1965. When they tore down the hotel . . . [*He grabs his bike, joins the other boys, they carefully look outside to see if the coast is clear, and with their bikes leave . . .*]

[*Fade out.*]

END OF PLAY

THE BIG BOOM AT NOON

Lesley Anne Moreau

The Big Boom at Noon was first produced by F.U.D.G.E. Theatre Company as part of the Third Annual Short Play Fest at Next Door Theatre in Winchester, Massachusetts, on May 11 and 12, 2012. It was directed by Julia Fiske WoodThe cast was as follows:

MELANIE: Alaina Fragoso
LUCY: Megan Bergeron
DONNIE: Ben Sharton

The Big Boom at Noon was produced by Happy Medium Theatre Company, April 2015 as part of HMT presents Shh . . . A Night of Mysteries, Scandals, and Taboos. It was directed by Mikey DiLoreto. The cast was as follows:

MELANIE: Elizabeth Battey
LUCY: Kim Klasner
DONNIE: Noah Simes

CHARACTERS
MELANIE: *15 years old*
LUCY: *15 years old*
DONNIE: *15 years old*

TIME
The present day.

SETTING
A high school classroom. LUCY *is seated at a desk.* MELANIE *is pacing back and forth anxiously.*

MELANIE: Oh my God! Oh my God! I can't believe this!

LUCY: It's not that big a deal.

MELANIE: It totally is.

LUCY: Whatever.

MELANIE: Um, excuse me? You know who's responsible for the big boom at noon. That's huge.

LUCY: I guess.

MELANIE: You have to tell someone.

LUCY: I can't.

MELANIE: Why not?

LUCY: 'Cause I promised I wouldn't.

MELANIE: Seriously?

LUCY: It's a promise. I can't break it.

MELANIE: So?

LUCY: So, that's a huge deal. That means something. Like, remember the time you got food poisoning at Applebee's and then you vommed all over the shoe display in Wet Seal?

MELANIE: Shh! Not so loud!

LUCY: Well, you made me swear I wouldn't tell and I never did. Just like Donnie Polaski made me promise.

MELANIE: That's completely different.

LUCY: How?

MELANIE: Because my secret only hurts my reputation. I mean, if anyone heard about that, my social life would become nonexistent. But Donnie's secret could potentially hurt the entire school. So not the same thing.

LUCY: Yeah, but it's all just been threats so far.

MELANIE: So far. Until he finally snaps and it actually happens.

LUCY: You don't really think he'd actually go through with it, do you?

MELANIE: Are you kidding? He's one of those weird ROTC kids that keep to themselves and he never washes his hair and none of his clothes are even from this decade. He's just weird.

LUCY: So now anyone who's a little different is capable of blowing up the entire school?

MELANIE: Obviously not. I mean, the SPED kids couldn't.

LUCY: Real nice, Melanie.

MELANIE: C'mon, even you know it's true. And then there's that kid who sets up the media equipment in all the classrooms. I mean, she's a known geek and a total castaway on the Island of Misfit Toys, but she's completely harmless. But Donnie just has this look about him that reeks "psycho." Like, when he looks at people, it's like he's trying to harm them in his mind, do you know what I'm saying?

LUCY: No, that's only what you think—there's no valid proof behind it.

MELANIE: What exactly did he tell you?

LUCY: Mel . . .

MELANIE: You brought it up.

LUCY: Swear you won't say anything?

MELANIE: Yes.

[*Pause.*]

LUCY: He just told me that he was the one calling in the threats. He said he was the one behind the big boom at noon and I should stay out of school that day.

MELANIE: Oh my God!

LUCY: What?

MELANIE: He totally likes you!

LUCY: What makes you think that?

MELANIE: Telling you to stay home. He's like so protecting you.

LUCY: But nothing ended up happening.

MELANIE: Yet.

LUCY: And it's not like he told just me. There were messages about it all over the bathroom walls and all those notes that were getting passed around.

MELANIE: But only you got the personalized message. Do the math, Lucy.

LUCY: I think he just wanted to talk. The stuff he told me about his home doesn't seem right. Like potentially bad stuff.

MELANIE: That doesn't make it okay to blow up the whole school.

LUCY: In case you haven't noticed, the school is still standing. And I didn't say it was okay.

[*Pause.*]

MELANIE: Is something going on between you two that you're not telling me?

LUCY: No! God, why do you always have to assume it's that way with everything? We just sit together in English class. Everyone else makes fun of him, so I guess he just feels comfortable talking to me.

MELANIE: Then why the need to protect him?

LUCY: I'm not protecting him. I just feel sorry for him. It's really messed up how everyone treats him just 'cause he's not the poster boy for Abercrombie and Fitch.

MELANIE: Still, you need to tell someone.

LUCY: I can't. I promised I wouldn't tell anyone.

MELANIE: But you told me.

LUCY: That's different. You're my friend. Have you ever known a secret that was so big, so huge, that you just had to tell someone, otherwise, you'd explode? Like, this secret is so powerful that it takes hold of your life and the only way you can take back control of your life is to get rid of that secret by telling someone else?

MELANIE: But now you're an accessory if you don't tell.

LUCY: What's to tell? We had a little scare but it's over.

MELANIE: They're doing locker searches; this is so not over. Look, not that I didn't appreciate the extra day of midterm studying we got when administration sent us home, but Donnie Polaski is the type to go postal at any moment, and when that happens, innocent people like you and me get hurt. You gotta tell Avery what you know.

LUCY: But . . . snitches get stiches.

MELANIE: This is not criminal warfare. What you know could save the entire student body from a lot of danger.

LUCY: I know but . . .

MELANIE: But what?

LUCY: It would be like betraying Donnie. It seems like a lot of people in his life have let him down. His parents don't seem to care about him, he has no friends. Do you know he's gone to Mr. Avery's office six times about the bullying and it's only gotten worse? I don't want to be added to the list of people who've let him down.

MELANIE: But he needs help of the mental variety. You'd be doing everyone a favor, including Donnie Polaski.

LUCY: He won't get the help he needs. Everyone will jump to conclusions and automatically assume the worst. They'll just throw him in some juvie detention center 'til he's eighteen and then even after that, who knows?

MELANIE: Better than people getting hurt . . . or worse.

LUCY: I can try talking to him.

MELANIE: 'Cause that's gonna do a hell of a lot.

LUCY: It's better than going behind his back.

MELANIE: If you say so.

LUCY: You wouldn't want me going behind your back and telling on you without at least some sort of warning first.

MELANIE: Well the worst thing I've done around here is stolen a few chocolate bars from the school fundraiser, not exactly a felony offense.

[*A figure suddenly appears lurking in the doorway.*]

MELANIE: What do you want?

[DONNIE *enters. He is also 15 and has long, chin length, greasy hair, and is wearing boots, baggy jeans, and an oversized army jacket that may have belonged to his grandfather.*]

DONNIE: I need to talk to Lucy for a second.

MELANIE: Well, well, well. I'll be out in the hallway, Lucy.

[MELANIE *exits, intentionally shoulder checking* DONNIE *on the way out.*]

LUCY: Don't mind Melanie. It's probably her time of the month or something. [*Pause.*] Everything okay?

DONNIE: So, I know there's been a lot of talk before, but the big boom at noon's really happening tomorrow.

LUCY: Not this again. Look, you really scared everyone but it's over.

DONNIE: It's not even close to being over. You need to stay home tomorrow.

LUCY: I've already cried wolf so many times to my parents, they're not going to believe it again. They even said so.

DONNIE: Tell them you heard from me. That I finally have the ammo and weapons to get the job done.

[*Pause.*]

LUCY: Please tell me you're joking.

DONNIE: No, it's for real this time.

LUCY: You can't, though. Think of how many people you'd be hurting, including yourself. Donnie, please—

DONNIE: No! It has to be done.

LUCY: Donnie, you should really, really think this through.

DONNIE: I already have. None of these people give a damn about me. They treat me like crap. Remember when Jordan Ricard and Matt DeSousa threw me in the dumpster behind the auditorium? I told Avery about it, and he said he couldn't suspend them because the football team needed them for Regionals. So much for the school's zero-tolerance-for-violence policy.

LUCY: That's awful and I'm sorry it happened to you. But Donnie, that's three people out of a school of like, seven hundred.

DONNIE: You're the only one here that's ever gone out of their way to be nice to me. You're my only friend here.

LUCY: But, other than English class, I don't really see you.

DONNIE: Yeah, but you at least talk to me and you're always nice. Do you remember that day you gave me a pen in class?

LUCY: No.

DONNIE: I didn't have one because Jordan snuck up behind me in the hallway beforehand and took all my pens and pencils out of my backpack. He wouldn't give them back. I ended up being late to class, and I got detention for it. I was so mad, but you let me have one of your pens and that made me feel better. It was a red sparkly gel pen. I love that pen. Jordan and Matt made fun of me for having a sparkly pen, but what do those idiots know? That was one of my favorite days 'cause you made me feel better.

LUCY: I don't remember. I mean, it was only a pen.

DONNIE: But it was a pen you gave me, when I needed one. Plus the sparkles remind me of you. You always write with sparkly pens.

LUCY: I'm glad I could help.

DONNIE: You treat me like a person instead of a plague. That means a lot.

LUCY: It's the least I can do.

DONNIE: I trust you Lucy, so please don't say anything.

[*Pause.*]

LUCY: Okay.

[DONNIE *starts heading for the door.*]

DONNIE: And promise me you won't come in tomorrow. I mean it.

[DONNIE *runs out. A few seconds later* MELANIE *reenters.*]

MELANIE: What did freakshow want?

LUCY: You shouldn't call him that.

MELANIE: Are you okay?

LUCY: I don't know.

MELANIE: Why? What's going on?

LUCY: Whatever you do, you can't come to school tomorrow.

MELANIE: Are you serious?

[LUCY *nods. Lights out.*]

END OF PLAY

THE BULLY'S EYE

Sam Affoumado

CHARACTERS

FORTUNA: *15 years old, female. A fortune-teller.*

JAMAL: *13 years old, male. A nerdy student who wears broken eye-glasses.*

BULLY: *14 to 15 years old, male. A physically imposing bully.*

TIME

The present.

SETTING

A fortune-teller exhibit at a school fair.

Scene 1

> *A school fair carnival exhibit. We hear carnival music in the background. The BULLY is hidden beneath a sheet and is standing perfectly still like a statue.*

FORTUNA: [*Hawking.*] Bully! Bully! Spin the bully! Step right up and see your world through the bully's eye! I am Fortuna, direct ancestor of the Roman goddess of Luck, Fortune, and Chance. Pay Fortuna and I will spin the bully and you will know your fate. Don't play the victim! See the world through the bully's eye.

> [*A young man enters. He is wearing broken eyeglasses that have been taped to hold them together. He watches FORTUNA as she continues to hawk:*]

Step right up and look the bully in the eye! See the future and find out what the bully has in store for you! Know how it feels to be a bully! Don't be shy! See the world through the bully's eye! [*Pause.*] Hey, kid! You gonna stand there all day? You're blockin' my view!

JAMAL: Sorry. Where should I stand?

FORTUNA: Don't ask me. I'm not a mind reader. I just spin the bully.

JAMAL: Oh. [*Pause.*] Why?

FORTUNA: Why what?

JAMAL: Why do you spin him?

FORTUNA: I get extra credit for working the fair. I bet you'd love to spin him.

JAMAL: Maybe. Why do you say that?

FORTUNA: 'Cause it looks to me like you've had a few run-ins with his kind. You've been bullied, haven't ya? Wouldn't you just love to spin him for a change?

JAMAL: [*Pointing to the sheet.*] Is . . . is that the bully?

FORTUNA: Yup. But it'll cost you. I can't give out no freebies.

JAMAL: How much?

FORTUNA: How much is it worth to you?

JAMAL: I don't know? A dollar?

FORTUNA: A dollar? Are you kiddin'? If you only wanna spend a dollar, then go over to the Kissing Booth. It's gonna take more than a buck to get a shot at this bully.

JAMAL: Why? What makes him so special?

FORTUNA: He's a bully without an audience. You know what that means? [*Whispering.*] He won't fight back. He has no reason to.

JAMAL: Oh. I don't know if I should be spending my money on—

FORTUNA: Look, kid, I'll make you an offer you can't pass up. Don't tell my teacher, but . . . I'll give you a free spin.

JAMAL: A free spin?

FORTUNA: Well . . . a limited spin, but if you like the outcome, you'll have to pay for the full experience. If you want the real spin, it may cost you everything you've got. What do you say, kid? Nothing ventured . . .

JAMAL: A free spin, huh? No strings attached?

FORTUNA: Absolutely none. Just remember. If you want more, it could cost you everything.

JAMAL: Okay. Deal! What do I have to do?

FORTUNA: Nothing! Just give me a sec and you'll get your free spin. [*She mumbles a few words as if she is chanting, and then she removes the sheet revealing the* BULLY, *who is facing upstage. When she smacks him on the back, we hear creepy, distorted music playing, and the* BULLY *slowly begins to spin.*]

JAMAL: Now what?

FORTUNA: Shhh! Just wait!

[*The* BULLY *stops spinning.*]

BULLY: You're a nerd. I hate nerds! I'm gonna bust your face! I'm gonna squash you like a bug! You little dirtbag! Four-eyed little wuss!

JAMAL: Oh, no.

FORTUNA: Come on, kid! Fight back! [*Whispering.*] He can't do anything to you, remember?

JAMAL: Oh, yeah. [*To* BULLY:] You better shut up. You . . . you big jerk! Yeah! That's what you are. Just a big, fat jerk!

[*Pause.*]

FORTUNA: That's it? That's all you've got?

JAMAL: I don't know. What else is there?

FORTUNA: Plenty!

JAMAL: Oh. You better watch out, or I'll—

FORTUNA: Sorry, kid. Time's up! [FORTUNA *covers the* BULLY *with the sheet.*] If you want more, you gotta pay up. Pay me and I'll give him a real spin—a spin you'll never forget.

JAMAL: I don't know. [*He giggles.*] It did feel good to yell back at him and not have to worry about the consequences.

FORTUNA: YOLO! YOLO!

JAMAL: What?

FORTUNA: You-only-live-once!

JAMAL: Oh, yeah. Okay. How much?

FORTUNA: Empty your pockets. It'll take all you've got.

JAMAL: All of it?

FORTUNA: Yup.

JAMAL: Okay.

[*He empties his pockets and* FORTUNA *begins to count it all, including the loose change.*]

FORTUNA: All right, kid. Now you'll get your money's worth. Step back!

SAM AFFOUMADO

[*She removes the sheet and mumbles a few words as if she is chanting, and then she smacks the bully on his back. We hear creepy,
distorted music playing as the* BULLY *slowly spins.*]

JAMAL: Now?

FORTUNA: Shhh! Just wait!

[*The* BULLY *stops spinning.*]

BULLY: Hey you! Fish face! You geek! Loser! Nerd! Nerdalator! I'm
gonna "f" you up! Just wait till I get you on the bus. Your ass is
grass!

[*Pause.*]

Come on and fight back! What are you gonna do about it, huh?
Huh? I'll bust you up!

JAMAL: Stop it! Stop it! Stop it! Why do you torture me every day?
What did I ever do to you?

BULLY: You exist! I hate your existence! I will always torture you.
Always! Until the day you die! Do us all a favor and just disappear!
Will 'ya?

JAMAL: No! I don't want to disappear. I have a right to be here.

BULLY: No, you don't! You're a little wuss and you have no rights.
It's my job to make your life a living hell.

JAMAL: Why?

BULLY: Because nobody likes you! No one will miss you! You're
a "hashtag" MISFIT! Do us all a favor and disappear! You got no
friends. You're a worthless piece of poop!

JAMAL: No, I'm not! I do have friends.

BULLY: Yeah? Where? Where are your friends? I beat the crap out
of you every day, and where are your friends? I choked you on the
bus and your friends cheered me on. Your friends cheered me on
when I busted up your smartphone and broke your glasses. Don't
you get it? You are the entertainment! You got no friends! You're
nothin' but a loser!

JAMAL: [*Whimpering.*] I . . . I . . . do have friends.

BULLY: Where? Where the hell are they?

JAMAL: On . . . on Facebook.

BULLY: [*Laughing.*] Facebook! Ha! What a joke!

JAMAL: It's not a joke! I have 587 friends.

BULLY: Oooh! Lots of friends! They're not your friends! They're just numbers. Did you ever meet any of them face-to-face? Huh? Large numbers of losers reaching out to other large numbers of losers! Like you! Probably got catfished! [*He laughs.*]

JAMAL: No! And I'm not a loser! I'm not. Leave me alone.

FORTUNA: Come on, kid, fight back! Get your money's worth. Get him!

JAMAL: You better stop bothering me or I'll . . . I'll—

BULLY: You'll what! What are you gonna do, you gaytard! Oooh, I'm shaking. Herb alert! Herb alert!

JAMAL: I'll do something bad. You'll see! You'll be sorry!

BULLY: Sorry for what?

JAMAL: For ruining my life! You ruin my life! Why do you do it? Why?

BULLY: Because you give me a reason to live.

JAMAL: I don't understand?

FORTUNA: He's nothing without you. Don't you get it? Go on! Tell him!

JAMAL: You're . . . you're nothing without me.

BULLY: Hey, wait a minute! That's not . . .

FORTUNA: That's it. Tell him!

JAMAL: It's true, isn't it? I'm the reason you exist. You're nothing without me. Ha! You're a nothing! A big, fat nothing!

FORTUNA: There you go!

BULLY: Hold on, you little tool!

JAMAL: You have no dreams. You have no passion. You're a noob!

BULLY: You better quit buggin'!

JAMAL: I'm telling the truth! The truth hurts, doesn't it? You're the "hashtag" MISFIT!

BULLY: No. That's a lie!

JAMAL: You can't exist without me. No one pays attention to you unless you're beating up on people like me. You draw a crowd because—

BULLY: You see? I draw a crowd—

JAMAL: Because they're afraid of you! They're afraid you'll turn on them. So they cheer you on, but they hate you. All of them. They really hate on you.

BULLY: No, they don't!

JAMAL: Yes, they do! And they think you're the real loser!.

FORTUNA: That's it, kid! Now you're killin' it.

JAMAL: You know what they say behind your back? They say you're nothing but an epic failure! You are a fugly, lame-ass, epic failure!

BULLY: Stop, or I'll . . .

JAMAL: You'll what? You're a social fruit fly! A bottom-feeder! An unwanted pest! You're nothin' but hype! Do us all a favor and go kill yourself! It would make the world a better place!

BULLY: Don't say that. You're hurting my—

JAMAL: Feelings? Gimme a break! You don't have feelings! You're not human! You're a hard-core hater! How can you have feelings? If I busted you open, I'd find nothing but crap! That's what you're made of! You stink! You're rotten to the core! You tard! You loser!

FORTUNA: Hey, kid. Take it easy. You're going too far. Gotta be careful. Because . . .

JAMAL: I'm just gettin' started! Just wait till I get you on the bus. I'm gonna bust your grill! Come on chickenshit, and fight back! What are you gonna do about it, huh? Huh? I'll bust you up!

BULLY: Why are you torturing me?

JAMAL: Because I hate you! Because you exist! I'm gonna ruin your life big time! I'll be doggin' on you wherever you go! I'm gonna be your worst nightmare! I'll get you in school! On the bus! In your neighborhood! At your job! You'll wish you were dead! Do you hear me? I'll make you wish you were dead! Or maybe, I'll just get rid of you myself!

[*We hear loud thunderclaps as the lights flicker, and then blackout.*]

FORTUNA: Bully! Bully! Spin the bully! Step right up and see your world through the bully's eye!

[*Lights up. The* BULLY *is hidden beneath the sheet.*]

Pay Fortuna and I will spin the bully and you will know your fate. Step right up, ladies and gentlemen, and look the bully in the eye! I dare you!

[FORTUNA *removes the sheet to reveal* JAMAL *who has now become the new* BULLY.]

See your future and find out what the bully has in store for you!

[*Blackout.*]

END OF PLAY

FIGHT OR FRIGHT

Kayla Cagan

Fight or Fright was workshopped, read, and produced with Fell Swoop Playwrights and assorted cast members in Los Angeles, California, in October of 2014.

CHARACTERS

MATT PETERSON: *15 years old. JON's older, more athletic brother. He's been in karate for years and appears very strong and tough. He's very popular in high school already.*

JON PETERSON: *13 years old. MATT's younger, nerdier brother. He's never really needed MATT for advice; he's smart enough to figure things out on his own. But when it comes to protecting himself in an after-school fight, he finally finds out that his brother doesn't just have muscles—he's got a big heart, too.*

TIME

The present. Nighttime.

SETTING

This play takes place in the Petersons' family bathroom, in front of the mirror. The bathroom counter has two sinks. MATT is standing in front of one of them, flossing his teeth. He can't help but check himself out, flexing his muscles, smiling like he would at a cute girl. He's goofing around. JON walks in on him.

JON: What are you doing?

MATT: Flossing, Bro. [MATT *begins flossing again.*] What's up?

JON: I need to brush my teeth.

MATT: So brush.

JON: Are you almost done?

MATT: Flossing? Yes. Brushing? No.

JON: You take a lot of time in here.

MATT: I've got to keep up my look, Bro.

JON: Whatever.

MATT: What's up with you?

JON: What do you mean?

MATT: What do you want?

JON: What?

MATT: You never come in here when I'm doing my thing.

JON: Well, I needed to . . .

MATT: If you need to go to the bathroom, just say so, dude.

JON: No. No, that's not it. If I needed to pee, I'd pee.

MATT: Well?

[MATT *starts to put toothpaste on his toothbrush.*]

JON: Wait.

MATT: What?

JON: Before you brush . . .

MATT: Dude . . .

JON: I need your help.

MATT: [*Laughing.*] With what? Brushing? Flossing? I thought Mom already covered that with you.

JON: Very funny!

MATT: What can I say?

JON: Never mind. You can't help me anyway. [JON *starts to leave the bathroom.*]

MATT: Whoa whoa whoa, Little Bro. What's going on?

JON: You wouldn't understand.

MATT: I was kidding, Bro.

JON: You're always kidding!

MATT: Okay, Captain Sensitive-o! What's your deal?

JON: I need . . .

MATT: Yeah?

JON: [JON *puts his own toothbrush in his mouth.*] I need your help with [*He mumbles.*] a fight.

MATT: Say what?

JON: Don't make fun of me.

MATT: How can I make fun of you? I didn't even hear you.

JON: Yeah, right.

MATT: Alright, weirdo.

[JON *pulls his toothbrush out of his mouth.*]

JON: FINE! I NEED YOUR HELP WITH A FIGHT!

MATT: [*Laughing.*] A fight? You? Who'd you make mad? Your computer science teacher?

JON: I knew you wouldn't take me seriously.

[JON *throws his toothbrush down on the sink.*]

MATT: Calm down! Calm down, Dude. Okay, tell me what's going on.

JON: Are you just going to make fun of me?

MATT: No guarantees.

JON: C'mon!

MATT: I'm just screwing with you, Bro! I'm not going to make fun of you. Tell me what's going on. For real.

JON: You know Eric Spartan?

MATT: Yeah.

JON: He wants to kick my butt after school.

MATT: Why? What'd you do? Hack his homework?

JON: I kissed Angela.

MATT: Angie Greenspan? NO YOU DIDN'T!

[MATT *holds his hand up for a high five but* JON *just looks at it.* MATT *picks up* JON*'s hand and makes him high-five him. It's awkward.*]

MATT: That's my bro!

JON: No, no it's not good, Matt. It was a mistake.

MATT: It's never a mistake to kiss Angie Greenspan.

JON: It is when you're not Eric and I'm not Eric. And as much as I told Eric it was a mistake and I didn't mean to and Angie didn't mean to, he won't accept it. He's told everyone he's fighting me after school. He's already tried to attack me online, but he's a joke. Not scared of him there, but I can't . . .

MATT: Fight-fight.

JON: Right.

MATT: So . . .

JON: I need you to show me some moves from your karate class. Something where if I get in trouble, I can get myself out of it.

MATT: You know I got your back, right, Jonny? I can meet you when the fight takes place. I can jump in. You can tag me in. You don't have to do this.

JON: You don't think I can?

MATT: It's not that. It's that Eric is a big dude.

JON: Yeah, he doesn't even look like he's in eighth grade.

MATT: I can help you out.

JON: I have to do this myself.

MATT: Why?

JON: Please don't make me explain this to you.

[*They look at each other, with the understood look between brothers.*]

MATT: Alright, man. If this is what you want, I'll teach you a few moves.

JON: Thank you.

MATT: First, you have to stand like this. Here, look in the mirror.

[MATT *and* JON *look out at the audience. The audience is "the mirror" they are looking into during the training sequence.*]

JON: [*Copying him.*] Like this?

MATT: That's right. Now bend your knees.

[JON *bends his knees to comic effect.*]

MATT: No, not like that! Like this.

[MATT *adjusts* JON *to the correct stance.*]

MATT: You have to look *and feel* relaxed. You're dead in the water if your knees and arms are locked. Understand?

[JON *nods.*]

MATT: Now, relax your shoulders.

[*Again,* JON *exaggerates his shoulder rolls.* MATT *tries not to laugh.*]

MATT: Calm down, dude. You're not getting a massage.

[JON *nods and shrugs his shoulders out.*]

MATT: Now, from your hips and waist, I want you to think about moving left or right. When I yell "Left," dodge left. When I yell "Right," dodge right, but only from your hips up. Get it?

JON: Got it.

MATT: RIGHT!

JON: Why are you yelling at me?

MATT: Huh? What? No, I'm not yelling at you. I'm giving you commands, like my Sensei Lee does.

JON: Oh, okay.

MATT: Let's try again. Ready?

JON: Ready!

MATT: Right!

[JON *dodges to the left stiffly and awkwardly. He makes a loud yelp as he does each dodge. It's nerdy and weird and funny.*]

MATT: Left!

[JON *dodges right hard and almost falls down.* MATT *helps* JON *regain his balance.*]

MATT: What's with the sound effect?

JON: What?

MATT: Don't you hear what you're doing?

JON: Not really.

MATT: Huh.

JON: What?

MATT: I have another idea.

JON: Like?

MATT: Have you heard of Fight or Fright?

JON: I think it's called Fight or Flight.

MATT: No, I know Fight or Flight. I'm talking Fight or Fright.

JON: What's that?

MATT: Instead of fighting, you make your challenger fear you. You put the fear of crazy in them. I think it may be the way you can win this fight.

JON: So what do I need to do?

MATT: You can scream, right? Like what you were doing when you were dodging just now?

JON: Like this?

[JON *lets out a wild and crazy scream. He really goes for it. It's funny, scary, and nuts all at once.*]

MATT: You're a genius. No wait, I'm a genius. That scream is genius! If you came running towards Eric Greenspan, he wouldn't know what to do! You looked like a mad ape!

JON: [JON *is hyped up and jumping around like an ape.*] So, I should just scream at him?

MATT: You dodge towards him and scream like that, I guarantee you Eric will run away crying like a baby.

JON: And if he doesn't?

MATT: Then you've got a big brother, Matt, and Matt doesn't let anyone pick on his little brother, even if his little brother kissed a girl he shouldn't have been kissing in the first place.

[MATT *gives a playful hit to his brother.* JON *is actually thrown off balance by it—not hurt, just surprised.*]

JON: Thanks for the lesson . . . Bro.

MATT: Anytime, Bro.

[JON *lets out one more crazy-animal scream and* MATT *is stunned at first, then cracks up.* MATT *holds up his hand for a high five and* JON *high-fives him correctly this time.* MATT *hands* JON *his toothbrush and, looking into the mirror, they both begin brushing their teeth at the same time.*]

END OF PLAY

HOLD FOR THREE

Sherry Kramer

CHARACTERS
SCOTTIE: *12 to 15 years old, female*
BARTEY: *12 to 15 years old, female*
ED: *12 to 15 years old, male*

TIME
The present day.

SETTING
SCOTTIE, BARTEY, *and* ED, *school friends, are at the beach, at the water's edge. The horizon exists on a line parallel with the top of the audience.* SCOTTIE *points at the horizon, excited.*

SCOTTIE: There—[SCOTTIE *is pointing at the moon, which has just started to rise.*] She's up—she's up. ED!! [SCOTTIE *grabs* ED *by the shoulders.*] This is it, Ed. You can do it! Take a big one! [ED *takes in a huge breath of air. She yells at* BARTEY.] Time!

BARTEY: This is ridiculous—he's not going to be able to hold his breath while the moon comes up.

SCOTTIE: Come on, come on—look at your watch.

BARTEY: Okay, okay. It is exactly—

[SCOTTIE *looks at her watch, and reports whatever time it actually is.*]
_____ and 17 seconds. . . . Let's subtract 5 seconds to adjust for operator error, shall we?

BARTEY: What do I care, Scottie? Really.

SCOTTIE: Okay, now, Ed—the first 30 seconds or so are easy. Just relax and save yourself.

BARTEY: [*Looking at* ED, *shaking her head.*] You're weird.

SCOTTIE: Adjusted time from start?

BARTEY: Uh . . . 23 seconds.

SCOTTIE: Okay. Allllllllllright.

[*Coaching sequences are spoken directly to* ED, *as excitedly as possible.*]

Now. I want you to imagine that you are in a megastar 3-D disaster film with Bruce Willis, Brad Pitt, and Angelina Jolie. You are underwater in—in a nuclear submarine. Angelina is trapped in the compartment where Polaris missiles are armed and ready to fly. You got to hold your breath long enough to get in, rescue her, disarm six missiles, and save the world from nuclear holocaust. Got that? [ED *nods, and mimes spinning open bulkheads, disarming missiles, etcetera.*] Well. That ought to take him a while. Time?

BARTEY: He's never going to make it.

SCOTTIE: Give me a break. It's almost a third of the way up.

BARTEY: A third? A third? His eyebrows just popped up.

SCOTTIE: The man in the moon does not have . . .

BARTEY: Well, if he did, that's what we'd—oooh, here come the eyes.

SCOTTIE: Time, damn it, time—I got a man here trying to do a job.

BARTEY: Fifty-three seconds.

SCOTTIE: Okay. Here we go. [*To* ED.] You're Anne Frank. Three storm troopers with boots polished to a shine hard enough to bounce laser beams enter the room. You're hiding in a pile of dirty laundry. One breath out of you—you'll feel the cold steel of their bayonets. [ED *crouches on the floor, his hands covering his head, keeping very, very still.*] Not bad, huh?

[ED *makes a mezzo-mezzo gesture with one hand.*]

BARTEY: [*Looking closely at* ED.] He's turning blue.

SCOTTIE: [*Looks carefully, too.*] He just didn't shave this morning, that's all.

BARTEY: And he's shaking, I think.

SCOTTIE: [*Looking at the moon.*] It's close to halfway, wouldn't you say?

BARTEY: Why is he shaking like that?

SCOTTIE: Oh, differences in temperature in the atmospheric layers, something like that I guess. Distorts the airwaves.

BARTEY: No, not the moon. Ed.

SCOTTIE: So he's shaking a little. Look—the bridge is up!

BARTEY: What?

SCOTTIE: Of his nose. Bridge is up, get it?

BARTEY: I hope he doesn't pass out or anything—I mean what if he hyperventilates in reverse or something. What if he forgets how to breathe?

SCOTTIE: [*As a narrator on a TV science program.*] It took the genetic ancestors of Ed Carmichael billions and billions of years to learn to use their lungs. [*As herself.*] Even Ed can't screw all that up in three minutes. Time!

BARTEY: One minute, 38 seconds.

SCOTTIE: And the boy is sweating bullets. I know you're gonna love this one, Ed. It's 1969. You're president of your university's SDS. The antiwar protest seems to be coming along fine when— TEAR GAS!!!! The pigs have just lobbed in the tear gas—one whiff and you're reduced to a slobbering flower child—you've got to hold your breath long enough to take over the dean's office—GO FOR IT!!!!! [*ED mimes running, choking on tear gas, fighting with policemen, etcetera.*]

Time?

BARTEY: One minute, 58.

SCOTTIE: [*Looking at the moon.*] Looks like we're getting into the mouth now. Ed—Ed, hang on, just a couple lips to go. [*ED indicates that he just can't go on.*] Ed—Ed—don't give up now—come on, come on, you can do it—all you have to do is pretend you're—pretend you're—GOD!!! Yes, you're God, and it's Day One of Creation. You've got a whole world of things to make before you get around to breathing the breath of life into Adam, so you hold it—you hold your breath for five days of creatures and firmament and shrubs— only you can do it, Ed, because you're GOD! [*ED is past making a rude response to this one. He struggles on. SCOTTIE is near hysteria.*] TIME!!!

BARTEY: Two minutes, 23.

SCOTTIE: THE HOME STRETCH!!! We're getting into the chin, now. You'll never *guess* what I've saved for the home stretch. [*ED struggles to his feet and stands, ready.*] You've been unjustly convicted of murder, and sentenced to the gas chamber. You're strapped in—when NEW EVIDENCE PROMPTS A PARDON FROM THE GOVERNOR—but—THE GAS PELLETS HAVE ALREADY BEEN RELEASED!!!!!! The guards are rushing to the door to save you—if only you can hold your breath till . . . [ED *pretends sitting in the chair, ripping off the restraining straps, going wild trying to hold his breath in the gas chamber.*] TIME!!!

BARTEY: Two minutes, 44 . . .

SCOTTIE: They're rushing to save you . . .

BARTEY: Clearing the chin now . . . [BARTEY *is now caught up in the excitement.*]

SCOTTIE: They're almost to the door now . . .

BARTEY: Just this much more to go—[*Makes an eighth of an inch with thumb and first finger, after measuring on the horizon.*]

SCOTTIE: They're at the door . . .

BARTEY: Two minutes and—you can do it, come on . . .

SCOTTIE: They're opening the door . . .

BARTEY: TEN . . .

SCOTTIE: No, it's stuck . . .

BARTEY: NINE . . .

SCOTTIE: They're using brute force . . .

BARTEY: EIGHT . . .

SCOTTIE: The guards have asked for help from . . .

BARTEY: SEVEN . . .

SCOTTIE: The people from the press . . .

BARTEY: SIX . . .

SCOTTIE: The reporters are throwing their weight around . . .

BARTEY: FIVE . . .

SCOTTIE: The door starts to give . . .

BARTEY: FOUR . . .

SCOTTIE: It starts to give . . .

BARTEY: THREE . . .

SCOTTIE: [*Looking at the moon rather than* ED.] Come on, come on, it's starting to give now . . .

BARTEY: TWO . . .

SCOTTIE: It's—it's—it's completely UP!!!!

    [ED *collapses on the floor.*]

BARTEY: ONE!!!! HE DID IT!!!! THREE MINUTES FLAT!!!

    [BARTEY *and* SCOTTIE *gaze at the moon for several seconds.*]

SCOTTIE: Beautiful, isn't it, Ed?

ED: [*Raises his head, looks at the moon for the first time.*] Yeah.

    [*Beat.*]

    [*Blackout.*]

END OF PLAY

I DID IT!

Elayne Heilveil

CHARACTERS

CARLY: *11 to 14 years old; a good student.*
SARA: *11 to 14 years old; CARLY's best friend.*

TIME

The present day.

SETTING

On a school day inside the girls' bathroom. CARLY *comes in agitated.* SARA *is primping in front of the mirror.* CARLY *stops in front of the mirror and stares at her face.*

CARLY: Oh my God, do I look different?

SARA: Mocha-Licious lip gloss?

CARLY: [*Shakes her head, no.*] Uh-uh.

SARA: Petal Pusher Pink blush?

CARLY: Uh-uh.

SARA: [*Squints to check her out.*] Milky Mauve shadow?

CARLY: I think I did it.

SARA: You did? [CARLY *shakes her head, no.*] I mean . . . you didn't? [*Beat.*] Do what?

CARLY: Say yes. I said it.

SARA: Okay. [*Beat.*] To what?

CARLY: To Gilbert Gottlieb.

SARA: Oh . . . my . . . God! The double G?!

CARLY: He asked me. And you know . . . [SARA *shakes her head like she doesn't.*] . . . before I knew what I was saying . . .

SARA: He asked you . . . [CARLY *nods.*] . . . out?

CARLY: [*Shakes head, no.*] Nah-uh.

SARA: To . . . the dance?

CARLY: Nah-uh.

SARA: For a kiss?

CARLY: I swore I wouldn't tell. I swore to Gilbert. And now I feel . . .

SARA: . . . slutty . . . ?

CARLY: . . . sick! I feel sick. I'm sorry. [*Pulls herself together.*] The only question is, do I evaluate multinumber expressions?

SARA: What?

CARLY: You know, complimentary and supplementary angles. And what would the measure of a missing angle be?

SARA: Carly!

CARLY: I mean there are variable expressions to represent a word problem, right? And then there's translation and reflection and . . .

SARA: Fine, if you don't want to tell me, I don't care.

CARLY: There are only three choices. Greater than, less than, or equal to, and I am . . .

SARA: . . . What?! Okay. Don't tell me. Just stand there. And I'll just . . . act it out and you just nod, or something. [*She wraps her arms around her back as if she's being hugged.*] "Oh Gil . . . Gil . . ."

CARLY: Sara! This isn't funny. I am so in trouble.

SARA: Like if your parents ever knew you'd be like dead or something funny?

CARLY: I kissed him!

SARA: Oh, my God! The double G?! I knew it! I mean, I could tell. You *do* look different.

CARLY: I mean his picture! I kissed his picture. In my locker. That's all I did. Okay, and then again, at Rachel Kruger's party. That's it! I blew one to him when he wasn't looking. I don't know why. Just to see what it would feel like maybe? And maybe someone saw me? And maybe they told Rachel? Who maybe told Dara. Who probably told Bradley. 'Cause they're like glued together. And he told Parker. 'Cause they're like on the team together. Which means the whole football team by now must know and . . . oh, I don't know how or who or why, but when I saw him in the hallway, coming towards me, and then he stopped.

SARA: He stopped? Gilbert stopped?

CARLY: And took my arm . . .

SARA: He touched you?

CARLY: And led me in the corner . . .

SARA: Which corner?

CARLY: Sara!

SARA: Sorry.

CARLY: And then he whispered [*Whispers.*] "Carly . . . Hey, Carly . . ."

SARA: He knew your name?

CARLY: "This is just for you," he said, "Like you and me . . . this is just between us, promise?"

SARA: I swear, on the life of my cat, not a soul, ever.

CARLY: No, that's what *he* said. "This is just between us, promise?" And I said, "Okay."

SARA: I'm going to pee. I mean, I'm feeling the pressure. I can feel it.

CARLY: That's okay. Never mind. I shouldn't . . .

SARA: No, No! I can hold it. Tell me!

CARLY: Okay, all right. But you gotta swear . . .

SARA: I swore! On my cat and all the little kitties she's giving birth to!

CARLY: Okay, okay. So, he leaned in closer . . .

SARA: Did you like . . . smell him?

CARLY: Sara! And he said, "Will you . . . could you . . . ?"

SARA: [*Nodding.*] Uh-huh . . .

CARLY: [*Lowers voice, like he did.*] . . . Do it?

SARA: [*Eyes widen.*] IT? Like, IT, IT?!

CARLY: [*Nods.*] It.

SARA: No way.

CARLY: Way. "All . . . of it," he said. I swear, that's what he said. Just like that. Will . . . you . . . do all . . . of . . . it.

SARA: In the hallway? [*Fans herself.*] I am so not breathing.

CARLY: And then he said that I was really smart . . .

SARA: . . . Uh-huh . . .

CARLY: . . . and really nice . . .

SARA: Well, sometimes.

CARLY: . . . and really good . . .

SARA: Really, REALLY good.

CARLY: . . . and he would like be forever . . .

SARA: . . . yours? The double G? Forever . . . ?

CARLY: . . . grateful. Forever . . . grateful.

SARA: Gilbert Gottlieb. Grateful? Huh. The double G? A . . . triple?

CARLY: So I said . . .

SARA: [*Shuts eyes—imagining.*] "Yes . . . yes . . . !" [*Opens eyes.*] You did, right? Or didn't? I can't remember.

CARLY: And I said . . . "Okay."

SARA: Okay.

CARLY: Just like that. [*Shrugs.*] "Okay." I mean my heart was pounding. But it slipped right out. Okay. And then I stood there. And nodded. And he said . . . "Cool." And started walking off. And then he turned. And then said, "And if you're real good at math, I'll let you do my English homework."

SARA: [*Stares at her with horror.*] He didn't.

CARLY: He did.

SARA: I need air.

CARLY: And then I heard like giggles. And Rachel and Dara and Tillie Johnson and Carrie Kramer and who knows who else were peeking around the corner, and . . . laughing. Like pointing and laughing, laughing. And I was . . . sick. Like I am . . . dying. Like as I speak . . . right now, [*Deep breaths.*] I think . . . I'm dying.

SARA: And I am . . . dying for you.

CARLY: I don't know how. I could have thrown the kiss to anyone. And I've always hid his picture in my locker. And the only one I ever told was . . .

[SARA *starts backing away.*]

SARA: I . . . I have to pee now.

CARLY: Sara . . . ? Sarafina . . . !

[SARA *stops. Doesn't turn.*]

SARA: [*Meekly.*] Yes?

CARLY: You didn't.

SARA: What? I didn't what?

CARLY: Tell someone? [*Beat.*] You told someone. Oh my God. You told them?!

SARA: I . . . just . . . had lunch with Tillie Johnson.

CARLY: . . . and . . . ?

SARA: And I said . . . Oh, I don't know . . . what I said. I was eating!

CARLY: You told Tilly? Who's friends with Rachel and Dara?

SARA: We were talking about our dream dates and she mentioned Gilbert and I said . . . Who wouldn't want to be with Gilbert Gottlieb? That's all I said. Then she said that Gilbert had this thing for Carrie Kramer and I said . . .

CARLY: You said . . . ?

SARA: I don't know! I can't remember.

CARLY: Sarafina!

SARA: . . . that you probably wouldn't like that?

CARLY: That I wouldn't like it if Gilbert had a thing for Carrie Kramer? That's what you said?

SARA: Well, you wouldn't.

CARLY: I can't believe it. My BFF and you said that?

SARA: I didn't say . . . I mean, it wasn't like I told her that you loved him! She said that.

CARLY: Tilly Johnson said I loved Gilbert Gottlieb!?

SARA: And I said . . . nothing. I swear. I said nothing.

CARLY: She said that. And you said nothing?!

SARA: I mean I said . . . something. I must have said . . . like, I don't know. Like . . . Yeah. Or, whatever. I swear, that's all I said. I was eating a tuna sandwich!

CARLY: How could you?

SARA: I was hungry?

CARLY: I need to be alone.

SARA: Like now, alone?

CARLY: Like, for the rest of my life, alone! Like, crawl in a hole, alone! Like, never be seen again, alone! So, you can go now. Just . . . leave me! Alone! And go now!

SARA: O . . . okay. [*Beat.*] Can I just go . . . [*Points to the stall.* CARLY *glares.*] Sorry. Never mind. I'll just . . . hold . . . that thought. [*Starts off. Stops and turns back.*] So . . . are you . . . like . . . going to do it?

CARLY: Yes. I am going to be dying.

SARA: I mean . . . his homework? [*Shrugs.*] 'Cause if you're gonna', square roots are due . . . tomorrow?

[CARLY *glares.* SARA *shrugs apologetically and rushes off.*]

END OF PLAY

IN THE FOREST OF GONE

Don Nigro

CHARACTERS
JUNE REEDY: *13 years old.*
LORRY REEDY: *12 years old; JUNE's sister.*

TIME
October of 1954

SETTING
The play takes place in the attic of the house of JUNE and LORRY's Aunt Molly Rainey, in Armitage, Ohio. The girls are surrounded by trunks, an old mirror, a bird cage, and old magazines. LORRY, who is smart, small, and wiry, sits in the attic reading a large old black book. JUNE, who is more physically developed and less nervous, finds her.]

JUNE: I knew you'd be up here. What are you always doing lurking up here in Aunt Molly's attic?

LORRY: I like the attic. It's like time-travel up here. These trunks are just stuffed full of the past. You open them up and you're someplace else. Old magazines. Old clothes. Everything smells like something else. I like that. [*Holding an old blanket up to JUNE's face.*] Here. Smell.

JUNE: Get that thing away from me. It's full of moths.

LORRY: They're not going to bite you. Except for the rare, carnivorous moths of central Gondwanaland.

JUNE: Where?

LORRY: It's in this book. It's a shame you never learned to read.

JUNE: I read. I just don't read all the time like you. I read like a normal person.

LORRY: You don't do anything like a normal person.

JUNE: Aunt Molly is looking for you.

LORRY: Aunt Molly can go eat worms.

JUNE: Lorry.

LORRY: What?

JUNE: You've been coming up here all the time ever since our mother left.

LORRY: So?

JUNE: She's coming back, you know.

LORRY: I come up here to read.

JUNE: You can't read downstairs?

LORRY: I can't concentrate with old people around. Uncle Clete is always blowing his nose or talking to the bird. And this is a really good book.

JUNE: Did you steal that?

LORRY: No, I didn't steal it. I borrowed it from Mr. Van Vogt's Curiosity Shop.

JUNE: Does he know you borrowed it?

LORRY: I'm not sure he even knows his name.

JUNE: Aunt Molly says we shouldn't be hanging around that place.

LORRY: I like it there. It's like the attic. It's full of wonderful, strange old things.

JUNE: She says Mr. Van Vogt has a couple of screws loose.

LORRY: So does our mother. I really like this book. It's by this obscure Romanian writer named N. J. Drago. It's about the lost continent of Lemuria. It takes place a long, long time ago, when there were just five continents: Atlantis, Lemuria, Hyperborea, Mu, and Gondwanaland. On Atlantis they worship science and reason, and Mu is run by sorcerers, and Hyperborea is way in the north where everybody is really depressed, and Gondwanaland is full of savage jungles and impossibly ancient ruins—but Lemuria is my favorite, because that's the place where all the artists and musicians and acrobats and actors and people like that come from. And the Lemurians send these acting companies out all over the world, and they have all these adventures on the other continents, even though in Atlantis everybody thinks doing theater is a foolish waste of time, and in Hyperborea some of the actors freeze to death, and Gondwanaland has wild animals that eat them, and on Mu, the penalty for being caught doing theater is to be cut up in pieces like a cucumber.

JUNE: So why do they go to these horrible places?

LORRY: Because they're actors. Actors always go to horrible places.

They've just got to keep moving. Like our mother. Only they have brains. And they're not insane. Well, some of them are insane. But they're insane in a good way.

JUNE: Our mother is not insane. She's just restless.

LORRY: She's out of her mind. She's crazier than Mr. Van Vogt, and he's got his dead wife stuffed upstairs watching television.

JUNE: That's just a rumor.

LORRY: He thinks aliens are communicating with him through his radio, and he's still not as loony as our mother.

JUNE: She's just troubled.

LORRY: Well, so am I. I can see how she might get sick of us, but how could she run off and leave Ben like that? Ben is just a little kid. He doesn't understand. This is going to mess him up for his whole life.

JUNE: It's not going to mess him up.

LORRY: She messes everybody up. Our father hung himself in the barn because of her.

JUNE: That's not her fault.

LORRY: Of course it was her fault. I've been living with her my whole life, and I want to hang myself in the barn.

JUNE: You don't want to hang yourself in the barn.

LORRY: I want to hang myself someplace. I think I saw the panther.

JUNE: What panther?

LORRY: People have been seeing a panther all over town. Up at Grim Lake. Up by the Indian Caves. There's a panther loose around here.

JUNE: We don't have panthers in Ohio.

LORRY: We could have panthers.

JUNE: You're crazy.

LORRY: Don't call me crazy.

JUNE: Don't get upset.

LORRY: I'm not upset.

JUNE: She's coming back.

LORRY: She's not coming back, because she's crazy. But I'm not crazy. And I don't want to be like her. I don't want to be anything like her. I don't want to look like her or talk like her or think like her or do anything like her.

JUNE: You're not anything like her.

LORRY: I'm nervous like her. And I can't stop talking like her. And I see panthers.

JUNE: You don't see panthers.

LORRY: I saw the panther. In the dark. It was in the dark. Waiting. At the back of the house. In the poison ivy. Two red eyes in the dark.

JUNE: That was a dream.

LORRY: It wasn't a dream. [*Pause.*] What if I am crazy?

JUNE: You're not crazy.

LORRY: But what if I am? It runs in the family. Our father hung himself in the barn. Our mother is always running off to God-knows-where.

JUNE: Everything is going to be fine.

LORRY: Don't tell me everything is going to be fine. Everything is not going to be fine. That's the stupidest thing I've ever heard in my life. When in the entire history of the world has everything ever been fine? You want to know who's really crazy? People who keep telling you everything is fine. Those people have definitely not been paying attention.

JUNE: Well, what am I supposed to say to you? I never know what to say to you.

LORRY: Most of the time you don't say anything. You just sit there looking mysterious and beautiful and all the boys drop over dead.

JUNE: I'm not like you. I don't need to talk about everything.

LORRY: I don't need to talk about anything. Just the things that really make me mad.

JUNE: Everything makes you mad.

LORRY: Well, everything is stupid. Everything in this town is stupid. Everything in my life is stupid. And our mother is insane. And she just ran off and abandoned us with no explanation at all. Like we were nobody. Well, I'm not nobody. I'm somebody.

JUNE: I know you're somebody.

LORRY: Sometimes I come up here and I'm scared to look in that old mirror because I'm afraid I'll look in there and there won't be anybody looking back at me.

JUNE: That's not going to happen.

LORRY: In this book, in Gondwanaland, there's a forest, called the Forest of Gone. And in the Forest of Gone, everybody who ever went away from you is there. You go into that forest and they're all there, all the ones who abandoned you, that you thought you were never going to see again. And at first you're so happy to see them, and you want to talk to them and ask them why they went away from you, what they were thinking or what you did wrong. But they won't look at you. They just look right through you. And you realize they're looking at somebody else. Somebody behind you that you can't see.

JUNE: She comes back. She goes away, but she comes back. She always comes back.

LORRY: I don't want her to come back.

JUNE: Yes you do.

LORRY: No, I don't, because if she comes back she's just going to leave again. She comes back and she gets you to like her again and then just when you start to trust her she goes away again, and she keeps doing it over and over again until she's made you as crazy as she is. So don't try and tell me it's going to be all right because it's not all right and it's never going to be all right because I'm crazy like she is, and I'm going to grow up and betray the people who love me and run away from everybody who cares about me, and I'll end up in the Forest of Gone. And you'll come to see me there, and I'll just look right through you. I'll just look right through you. Because I'll really be looking at somebody who isn't there. Because the person we love is always the person who isn't there. That's how we know they're the person we love. Because they're not there.

JUNE: I'm here. I'll always be here. I promise.

LORRY: You can't promise that. You don't know that.

JUNE: I'm here now.

LORRY: Yes, but I'm not. I'm in the Forest of Gone.

[JUNE *puts her arms around* LORRY *from behind and holds her.*]

JUNE: Look in the mirror.

LORRY: I don't want to look in the mirror.

JUNE: Look in the mirror. See? See that girl? She's smart, and funny, and very stubborn, and very strong, and she feels things very deeply, and that's a good thing. It hurts, but it's a good thing. You are going to grow up, and you're going to love people, and people are going to love you, and some of them will go away, because maybe everybody and every thing you love goes away. So you love them as much as you can while they're here. And that's all you can do. Because that's all there is.

[*Pause.*]

LORRY: But what if I really am crazy?

JUNE: Then we'll be crazy together.

[*They look in the mirror. The light fades on them and goes out.*]

END OF PLAY

JUST YOUR IMAGINATION

Lesley Anne Moreau

Just Your Imagination was first produced by Salem Theatre as part of the Eighth Annual Moments of Play Festival in Salem, Massachusetts, from July 9 through 13, 2014. It was directed by Chuck Baker and featured the following cast:

KATIE: Nicole Bauke
ANGELA: Julia Short

CHARACTERS
KATIE: *6 years old, a girl with a big imagination.*
ANGELA: *13 years old,* KATIE*'s older sister.*

TIME
The present day.

SETTING
The play takes place in a children's playroom. ANGELA *is seated at a table playing a board game with her sister,* KATIE.

ANGELA: You cheated!

KATIE: I did not.

ANGELA: Yes you did. You were supposed to move back three spaces and you didn't.

KATIE: That's because I got a spell card that reversed me, so I'm safe this time around. I only have to go back if it's the same number as me—I'm six, not three.

ANGELA: Sure, just like how you froze me two turns ago. You're just making up your own rules as you go along.

KATIE: I can't help it if I'm so good at winning.

ANGELA: No, but you can do something about that imagination. I won't play with you anymore if you don't follow the rules.

KATIE: But rules are boring, just like you.

ANGELA: Now I'm boring?

KATIE: Yeah, 'cause you play by the rules.

ANGELA: Nothing wrong with that.

KATIE: Yeah-huh. It's like the most boring thing ever.

ANGELA: Rules are meant to be followed.

KATIE: Bo-ring! You should break the rules tonight.

ANGELA: How?

KATIE: Sleep in my room with me!

ANGELA: Why?

KATIE: Because there's a monster under my bed. His name is Nigel and he's orange and scaly and has seven huge, giant fangs.

ANGELA: There's no such thing as monsters.

KATIE: Yeah-huh.

ANGELA: Not-uh. It's just your imagination.

KATIE: I know what I saw.

ANGELA: You Silly Billy. That's just your mind playing tricks on you.

KATIE: Well, if you sleep in my room we can play princesses and you could be the Queen Fairy Princess on High who slays all the monsters.

ANGELA: We can play princesses any time.

KATIE: But it's not the same. It's more fun at night 'cause we can play with flashlights and my glow-in-the-dark wings, and we can have a tea party in the closet and pretend our kingdom is fighting a battle outside and after tea we can join and kill all the monsters.

[*She pretends to sword-battle an imaginary monster.*]

ANGELA: You and your imagination.

KATIE: Angela?

ANGELA: What?

KATIE: Do you like Gary?

[*Pause.*]

ANGELA: Why do you ask?

KATIE: I don't know. I guess 'cause you've been kind of weird since he moved in with us.

[*Pause.*]

ANGELA: How so?

KATIE: You stay after school way later all the time now. You always say you're at the library, but that's a lot of time at the library. You never talk at dinner anymore. You don't talk about school either. Or have any of your friends over. Know how I know? You never kick me out of your room anymore.

ANGELA: You heard Mommy—it's going to be a huge adjustment for all of us. But she's happy with him and that's what matters most.

KATIE: But Angela . . .

ANGELA: What?

KATIE: I saw something.

[*Pause.*]

ANGELA: Whatever it was, it was probably nothing. Just your imagination again.

KATIE: I know it was for real.

[*Pause.*]

ANGELA: What did you see?

KATIE: The other night I got up from bed 'cause I had to go bathroom, and I saw Gary go in your room. Why did he do that?

ANGELA: I told you. It was just your imagination.

KATIE: I know when I see things for real and when I pretend them. This was for real 'cause I wasn't even a bit sleepy yet 'cause I had to go bathroom so bad.

ANGELA: It was nothing.

KATIE: But why did he go in your room?

ANGELA: Did he see you?

KATIE: Not-uh.

ANGELA: Good.

KATIE: You still haven't told me why.

ANGELA: I needed help with my homework.

KATIE: But it was real late at night. You never do homework that late.

ANGELA: It was algebra. We're learning it this year and I'm having problems with it. It's really, really hard. It's keeping me awake.

[*Pause.*]

KATIE: Does Mommy know?

ANGELA: She works the night shift now—it's not like she can help me.

KATIE: But does she know you're not doing good in school?

ANGELA: No, I don't want to worry her.

KATIE: But she's gonna find out. I don't want you to get punished.

ANGELA: I'm not going to get punished. Just don't say anything, all right?

KATIE: Why?

ANGELA: Because, it could hurt Mommy's feelings. And you don't want to do that, right?

KATIE: I guess not.

ANGELA: And that's why you're not going to say anything.

KATIE: Okay.

ANGELA: Katie, swear you won't say anything. Mommy's been through a lot and I just want her to be happy.

[*Pause.*]

KATIE: I swear.

ANGELA: Good. Let's finish our game.

KATIE: Okay.

[KATIE *picks up the dice. She does not roll them.*]

KATIE: Angela . . .

ANGELA: What?

KATIE: But still . . . about Gary . . .

ANGELA: Katie, it's fine.

KATIE: I want you to sleep with me tonight.

ANGELA: No.

KATIE: But why not?

ANGELA: Because, you're a big girl. You can sleep by yourself.

KATIE: Please!

ANGELA: Katie, you have to.

KATIE: But I don't wanna!

ANGELA: Too bad.

KATIE: Why can't you sleep in here?

ANGELA: Because this is your room. I have my own.

KATIE: But you used to sleep in here all the time before Gary came.

[ANGELA *grabs* KATIE *by the shoulders.*]

ANGELA: Listen to me. In life sometimes we have to follow the rules even if we don't like them. But rules can protect you, keep you safe. It's not like playing a game where you can cheat or just end it if you're losing. I'm going to give you rules right now and you have to promise me you'll follow them and that you won't say anything to anyone, no matter what, okay?

KATIE: Okay.

ANGELA: When it's time for you to go to bed, you stay in your room, no matter what. If you have to go to the bathroom, don't.

KATIE: But what if I wet the bed? I don't want to do that.

ANGELA: If you do, just tell me in the morning and I'll clean it up.

KATIE: Why would you do that?

ANGELA: Just trust me, please. Every night you need to put your desk chair under the doorknob too. It'll help keep the monsters out.

KATIE: Okay.

ANGELA: The last and most important rule—you can't tell anybody what you saw, ever. Not Mommy, not your friends, not your daddy, no one. Understand?

KATIE: Why not?

ANGELA: Because . . . bad things could happen. I could get sent away to live with an evil witch lady who makes me clean all the time and you'd go live with your daddy for always and I'd never see you again, ever. Do you want that to happen?

KATIE: No!

ANGELA: Then this has to be our secret.

KATIE: Okay.

ANGELA: Okay, then you have to promise me you'll follow the rules.

KATIE: I promise.

[*Pause.*]

ANGELA: Thank you.

[KATIE *looks at* ANGELA *for a beat.*]

KATIE: Angela, do you need a fairy godmother?

ANGELA: I think so.

KATIE: Don't worry. I'll be yours.

[ANGELA *hugs* KATIE *tightly. Lights out.*]

END OF PLAY

MARKERS

Cory Terry

Markers received its World Premiere at American Globe Theatre in New York City on April 22, 2013. It was directed by Stephen Cedars, and the cast was as follows:

MANDY: Emma Wallach
MAX: Ben Radcliffe

CHARACTERS
MANDY: *10 years old.*
MAX: *12 years old,* MANDY*'s brother.*

TIME
Early afternoon on Christmas Eve. The present.

SETTING
MANDY *is seated on the grass next to a high white fence in her back-yard in Westchester County, New York. She wears oversized red gloves that clash with her knitted scarf and heavy wool peacoat. She's looking for something. After a few beats,* MANDY *begins calling out for her friend.*

Note: A forward slash ("/") indicates overlapping dialogue.

MANDY: Briiice!

> [MANDY *listens for a beat before hearing something and running across the yard.*]

MANDY: Are you there, Brice? I miss you, buddy.

> [MAX *enters from the house, wearing jeans and a thin windbreaker. He approaches* MANDY *tentatively.*]

MAX: What're you doing out here?

MANDY: Get away from me, Max.

> [*She walks to the opposite side of the yard.*]

MAX: I'm out of time-out now.

> [*He looks back to the house, where an unseen mother prompts him.*]

MAX: I'm sorry I punched you, Mandy.

> [*She eyes him for only a moment.*]

MANDY: It's okay.

MAX: Mom says if we don't fight again we can both open a Christmas gift tonight.

MANDY: I wasn't fighting. / You—

MAX: Yeah-huh! You hit me first and you always get everything . . .

[*He glances again toward the offstage mother and thinks better of arguing. Beat.*]

MAX: Where's / Dad?

MANDY: Where's Brice?

MANDY: Dad left to get us presents.

MAX: When did he leave?

MANDY: I dunno. When you were in time-out?

[MAX *is upset.* MANDY *notices and crosses to him, trying to make peace.*]

MANDY: I *hate* Christmas Eve mass. It's sooo long.

MAX: We didn't even have to go until you came along.

[MANDY *sticks her tongue out at him and resumes her search.* MAX *rubs his hands together.*]

MAX: It's so cold out here.

MANDY: Where're your gloves?

MAX: Mom says she has to get me some new ones.

MANDY: Do you know where Brice is?

MAX: [*Smiling at her. Innocent.*] When was the last time you saw him?

MANDY: I dunno. Bedtime last night? I was supposed to go with Mom when she took him to the vet this morning, but I don't think she went 'cause his crate isn't in the truck.

MAX: I'm not supposed to tell you.

MANDY: Shut up—tell me what?

MAX: [*A beat, with some pleasure.*] Brice is dead.

MANDY: Don't lie. Where is he?

MAX: He died. This morning. When you were sleeping.

MANDY: Shut up, Max! Where's my dog?!

MAX: Mom and Dad didn't want me to tell you. 'Cause of Christmas. But I saw him.

MANDY: [*Starting to believe.*] I don't believe you! [*Yelling.*] Mom!

MAX: Dad knew I could handle it, because I'm older, but he said, "Don't tell your little sister—she'll get upset."

[MANDY *starts crying and heads for the house.*]

MANDY: Mom!!!

MAX: Do you wanna see him?

[MANDY *turns back to him. Her wailing recedes into periodic sobs as she nods "yes." He leads her to the high white fence and swings the gate open. She peers through the opening and her wailing returns for a moment.*]

MAX: I told you. [*Beat.*] Dad dug the hole and Mom put him in the sack. She said I could write a poem or something, to put in with him, but I didn't want to.

MANDY: I want to.

MAX: The sack's all closed up now. So the possums won't get to him.

MANDY: But he's my dog!

[MAX *hesitantly puts an arm around her.*]

MAX: He was old, Mand. [*Beat.*] And he was my mom's dog.

MANDY: [*Breaking away from him.*] You're crazy. Mom knows he's my dog.

MAX: Not your mom. Dad got Brice with my mom, before she died. So, really, he was my dog.

MANDY: But they gave him to me. And you didn't love him. He was my buddy.

[*She peers into the grave.*]

MANDY: I don't like him here. In a hole.

MAX: [*Unaffected.*] C'mon, it's just a dog. [*Off her reaction.*] Dad'll cover him up. [*She's horrified. He sighs.*] How 'bout we put up a tombstone for him?

[MANDY *nods.* MAX *looks around the yard and finds a big rock.*]

MAX: Help me move this.

[*They struggle to lift the rock together and haul it across the yard, eventually placing it on the other side of the high white fence.*]

MAX: There. Now we'll always know where he is.

MANDY: Thanks, Max.

[*She holds his hand as they look at the grave for a long moment.*]

MAX: What if he didn't die, Mand? What would you do with him if he was still alive?

MANDY: I'd take care of him. Make sure he slept in my bed every night. And give him people food at the table, even if Mom told me not to. He'd never have to take a bath. And he could kiss my face all day long—I wouldn't even push him away. [*Beat. Remembering.*] And I'd rub his tummy. I'd be his best buddy.

[*They stand in silence for a few beats.* MAX *gets uncomfortable and steps away from her. He rubs his hands together and breathes into them.*]

MAX: I can see my breath. [*Beat.*] Hey, when it's cold like this, do you think you can see farts in the air?

MANDY: I dunno. [*Grinning.*] Have you seen mine? 'Cause I've been farting this whole time.

[*She laughs.*]

MAX: You're gross!

[*He playfully shoves her away from him and toward the grave.*]

MANDY: I couldn't help it.

[*Her smile fades as she looks back into the grave.*]

MAX: It's too bad we don't have any flowers for him.

MANDY: Yeah. [*Beat.*] I still have this.

[*She removes a glove and shows him the drawing on her hand.*]

MANDY: It's a real nice flower you drew. I'm not gonna wash it off.

MAX: Nah, we got those washable markers. It'll scrub off when you get your bath.

MANDY: I'm gonna keep it. I won't let Mom wash it off!

MAX: Suure . . .

[*Two beats.*]

MANDY: Hey, Max. What about your mom? What would you do if she was still alive?

MAX: I don't know.

MANDY: C'mon! No one tells me anything about her.

MAX: If she was still alive . . . [*Thinking.*] We'd still be in California. As a family. Me, her, Dad. We'd spend Christmas Eve at Grandma's house instead of going to church. And she'd make a real dinner. Fried shrimp and lasagna and turkey. Not cold cuts and Costco frozen meatballs like your mom makes.

MANDY: I like the meatballs!

MAX: The day after she died, Dad said, "You have a sister, and we're gonna go live with her and her mom in New York." Just like that. What about my mom? She's buried in California and I can't even go see her now. But I'll get to see this stupid dog every day.

[*He kicks dirt into the grave and turns on her.*]

MAX: You just had to take everything, didn't you?

MANDY: I didn't take / anything—

MAX: My gloves, my dog, my dad!

MANDY: I didn't. He's my dad, too!

MAX: He's not! No one wanted you!

MANDY: Shut up, Max! You said we were buddies.

MAX: I lied.

[*He takes a couple of steps toward the house.*]

MANDY: [*Pleading.*] Don't say that! Mom always said I had a brother. But she told me we'd never meet you. [*Crossing to him.*] I always wanted a big brother. And Mom said you'd take care of me. That you'd make sure nothing bad happened to me.

MAX: She lied, too. Have fun with your buddy.

[*He advances on her and shoves her through the gate and into the grave. She lets out a mix of screaming and crying as* MAX *starts back for the house.*]

MANDY: Max! I'm stuck! Help me, Max.

[MAX *stops and turns back to face the fence. He enjoys her pain. Her cries grow softer.*]

MANDY: Please, Max. I think I broke him. I'm scared.

[MAX *is torn, but after several beats he crosses back to the grave and pulls her out. She's still crying when she slaps him. After a few more beats she composes herself.*]

MANDY: Why'd you do that?

MAX: I don't have to take care of you.

MANDY: Yes you do! Ya know it's not my fault you moved here. And it's not my fault your mom died. And I'm sorry they gave me your dog, Max. I didn't know!

[*She rips off her gloves and throws them at him.*]

MANDY: And take these! I don't want them. And I don't want your stupid drawing.

[*She wipes some tears from her face and uses them to scrub the drawing from her hand. He tries to stop her, but she breaks free.*]

MANDY: Stay away from me!

[*She exits to the house. After a couple of beats,* MAX *picks up the gloves and puts them on. He walks over to the grave and kneels. After a few more beats:*]

MAX: You didn't wanna move here either, did ya, Brice? You remember what it was like to have a real family. With nice weather and Mom. [*Breaking down.*] Mandy didn't mean to hurt you, buddy. It was my fault. I pushed her onto you. Are you okay? I'm sorry. I'm so sorry, buddy.

[*He tucks his head between his knees and sobs.*]

END OF PLAY

SISTER AND BROTHER

Allan Havis

Sister and Brother was produced as a lab showcase in November 1977 at Yale Drama School with Tony Shaloub and Polly Draper. Directed by David Kaplan.

CHARACTERS
HOLLY: *age 15; a thin, forceful girl.*
TED: *age 12; a pale, recessed boy.*

TIME
The present day.

SETTING
HOLLY *and* TED *are home alone in a suburban house on a cold evening in mid-October.*

HOLLY: [*Forcing* TED*'s head with a headlock.*] Look, Ted!

TED: No!

HOLLY: It's real.

TED: Let go, you're hurting me.

HOLLY: First, tell me what you see.

TED: Vampires.

HOLLY: What else?

TED: Zombies.

HOLLY: What else, Teddy?

TED: [*Breaking away.*] I want to play ball.

HOLLY: No one's stopping you.

TED: Why did you call me in?

HOLLY: I called you in?

TED: Nobody was on the phone. I don't like your games.

HOLLY: Don't you want to play cards?

TED: You shouldn't lie, Holly.

HOLLY: If I didn't lie, would we have any fun?

TED: Who's making dinner for us tonight?

HOLLY: I'll make dinner. Popcorn and beer.

TED: No.

HOLLY: What will Mom say! [*Pause.*] Know who likes me? Billy Sherman.

TED: He goes out with Beth.

HOLLY: So? He's cute.

TED: Am I cute?

HOLLY: Too cute, Ted. You scare the girls away. Dad followed me to the movies.

TED: Why?

HOLLY: I went with Rick. Dad doesn't like Rick.

TED: What happened?

HOLLY: Dad sat two rows back. We were making out. My blouse was open. I had that funny feeling, you know, when the ceiling comes down on you. He clobbered Rick. Like really clobbered him. Right between the shoulders.

TED: When?

HOLLY: Last weekend.

TED: How come you didn't get punished?

HOLLY: 'Cause I know how to handle Dad. Gonna see Rick to-night.

TED: Do me a favor.

HOLLY: What, little brother?

TED: Don't spook me no more. Stay out of my room.

HOLLY: Just curious.

TED: An hour in my room and who walks out of my closet . . . and when Kathy sleeps over, don't wake me at 3 a.m.

HOLLY: Kathy's got a crush on you. And she knows you play with yourself.

TED: I do not.

HOLLY: Under your quilt! Like you're doing circus tricks under a tent! Who's your best buddy?

TED: Why does Mom collect those shitty bowling trophies?

HOLLY: Why does she play bridge? 'Cause she's lonely. Dad's not lonely.

TED: How do you know?

HOLLY: 'Cause he tells me things. His out-of-town stories.

TED: Tell me one.

HOLLY: You know the convention story? Here's the convention story. You know what a call girl is? Doing it for money.

TED: Dad does it for money?

HOLLY: Dad does it for free. That's the convention story.

TED: I don't like October. Don't like Halloween. Don't like winter.

HOLLY: We should have summer all year and go to the beach every day, Ted. When I skip school alone, I feel sad.

TED: Where do you go?

HOLLY: Bars. The Hi Spot across the street from Starbucks. I don't get carded.

TED: Kids at school talk about you.

HOLLY: Good. What do you tell them?

TED: I say it's all true.

HOLLY: I need a cigarette. [*She finds a pack and an ashtray.*] Bette Davis is a horror.

TED: Whatever happened to Baby Jane?

HOLLY: Ask Joan Crawford. Ask Psycho Anthony Perkins.

TED: What's on tonight?

HOLLY: Boredom. Want to wrestle?

TED: No. [*She tackles him and overwhelms him.*] Get off me!

HOLLY: Going to pin you, you little asshole. Top dog. Say it!

TED: Underdog.

HOLLY: Come hug. [*They do.*] Your sister loves you, creep.

TED: Think Mom and Dad will get a divorce?

HOLLY: Any day now. Who will you go with?

TED: Mom. You?

HOLLY: Not Mom! You're just like her. Come with us.

TED: What about her?

HOLLY: She can die.

TED: You got that spooky look in your eyes.

HOLLY: So do you, Teddy boy. You're not that different from me.

TED: It's getting dark out. Let's put on the lights.

HOLLY: How about a séance? I'll get the candles.

[*She throws her hands over his eyes.*]

TED: I hate séances!

HOLLY: Too late. The spirits know.

[*Candles come out and are lit.*]

TED: I don't believe in spirits.

HOLLY: Like hell you don't!

TED: Holly! Holly! What are you going to ask them?

HOLLY: If Mrs. Zensler is going to have a baby.

TED: We know she is.

HOLLY: But it might be a blue baby.

TED: Turn on the lights!

HOLLY: Watch the candles. See Aunt Selma.

TED: Not Aunt Selma!

HOLLY: I see her. She's not dead. She's raking the backyard leaves. Dad's pinching her behind.

TED: Stop it.

HOLLY: I see little Teddy. All dressed in a crib. Not even two. In the hospital. You didn't know, did you?

TED: Know what?

HOLLY: You're adopted.

TED: Shut up!

HOLLY: Ask Dad. Mom won't say.

TED: I hate you, Holly.

HOLLY: I'm only telling the truth.

TED: I see something. In the flame. Holly's on her knees. Rick's standing. Soon Holly's crying.

HOLLY: Shut up!

TED: He only wants you this way.

HOLLY: I'll knock you out, Teddy.

TED: Who's going to make dinner?

HOLLY: Mom.

TED: When's she coming home?

HOLLY: I told you.

TED: Where's Dad?

HOLLY: On the road.

TED: Where's Mom, really?

HOLLY: In your room. Sleeping.

TED: In my room?

HOLLY: Go look.

TED: No.

HOLLY: Sometimes I just want her to disappear.

TED: I'm going out.

HOLLY: Oh, no you're not. You're not leaving me alone. [*As he walks away, she grabs his wrist.*] Sometimes I just want to scare you. In your sleep.

TED: I'll stay awake. Let go of my arm. I say, let go!

[*She lets go and kisses his cheek.*]

HOLLY: Where are you going?

TED: To the 7-Eleven store. I'll be back in an hour.

HOLLY: Don't leave me, Ted. I'm scared to be alone. No one's home. [*He waits a few seconds and continues to leave the room.*] Don't leave me, Ted! Don't! Don't!

END OF PLAY

SUNDAY GO TO MEETIN'

Shirley Lauro

Sunday Go to Meetin' was presented by the League of Professional Theatre Women as part of their Festival of Short Plays at St. Peter's Church in New York City on May 22, 1988. It was directed by director Lenore Dekoven and assistant director Adam Nadler. The cast was as follows:

SALLY: Karyn Lynn Dale
HESTER: Jil Geddes
SARAH: Olivia Mates

Sunday Go to Meetin' was presented by Actors Theatre of Louisville in its Short Orders Festival, opening May 26, 1986. Larry Deckel was the director. The cast was as follows:

SALLY: Stefanie Vogel
HESTER: Anita Adsit
SARAH: Helen Greenberg

CHARACTERS

SALLY SUE JONES: *12 or 13 years old. A country girl. Naïve but inquisitive. She has blonde hair, tied at the nape of her neck by her Sunday ribbons. She is wearing her Sunday dress, white or pastel, with white high-top shoes. She is a "good old-fashioned girl."*

HESTER BLOODWORTH: *14 or 15 years old. HESTER is also a country girl, but she is the town daredevil. She is coquettish, mischievous, and always gets into trouble. She is also blonde and is dressed similarly to SALLY SUE.*

SARAH WARSAVSKY: *15 years old. SARAH wears a babushka on her head and a long dark skirt with black stockings. She is Semitic, dark, and is dressed in the style of an Eastern European peasant. She has already been through much in her young life and seems much older, much different, and more worldly than the other girls.*

TIME

A Sunday morning in early autumn of 1905.

SETTING

The setting is on a road leading to the Baptist Church at the edge of a rural village in Iowa.

Note: Several Yiddish phrases are spoken by SARAH. English translations are included for reference. In the production, the actress speaks only the Yiddish words.

> *At rise: Lights come up on a country road leading to a Baptist church. A white picket fence lines the road marking off the church property. In the distance we hear parishioners singing liltingly, slowly . . .*

> *[Offstage voices can be heard singing:]*

"Give me that old-time religion

Give me that old-time religion

Give me that old-time religion

It's good enough for me.

It was good enough for Brother

It was good enough for Sister

It was good enough for Mother

And it's good enough for me—"

> [*Church is about to begin. As voices drift off,* SALLY *enters on her way to Sunday school. She carries a copy of the Bible. As she comes along,* HESTER *appears behind her, carrying a Bible too.* HESTER *has been running to catch up with* SALLY.]

HESTER: Psst! Sally? Sally Sue?

> [SALLY *stops and turns.*]

SALLY: Yes?

HESTER: [*Giggling.*] Wanna go for a little walk with me? Right now??

SALLY: It's Sunday, Hester.

HESTER: Well, don't I jist know it's Sunday? My Land!

SALLY: Well, I can't go for no walk! I'm almost late right now!

> [SALLY *starts on her way,* HESTER *trailing her.*]

HESTER: Not even for a little bitty ole walk?

> [SALLY *is giggling to herself.*]

SALLY: What kind of walk? I got to go to Sunday school—you do too!

HESTER: Oh—just a walk down the road, edge a town. Take about fifteen minutes is all—just to see the wonder a the Lord all around us to behold among other things!

> [HESTER *now starts off, leaving* SALLY *in her wake.* SALLY *runs to catch up.*]

SALLY: What other things?

> [HESTER *stops.*]

HESTER: Oh, things Billy Henderson has told me about.

SALLY: What kinda things he tell you about?

HESTER: [*Laughing.*] Oh now just look at you! Eyes about to bug out of your head with the curiosity, huh? Wanna come?

SALLY: What things has Billy Henderson told you about? Tell me and I'll go!

HESTER: Well—you know over to the edge a town—that old warehouse place where the Wilkins lived upstairs and stored their grain downstairs? That old spooky old tumbledown shack place?

SALLY: What about it?

HESTER: [*Casually.*] Well, there's a pack a Jews moved in there—

SALLY: [*Astounded.*] WHAT??

HESTER: [*Still casual.*] Opened up a apple stand out front Billy says.

SALLY: [*Can't believe this.*] JEWS??

HESTER: Mmm. Two, three families of 'em—all related—all lookin' jist alike, Billy says. See, they bought the place and is movin' in here! PERMANENT!

SALLY: HERE??

HESTER: They went right on down to Hawkins Law Office & Real Estate Ink and plunked hundreds an hundreds a dollars down cash! Mr. Hawkins said he couldn't hardly believe his eyes how their men folks jist kept pullin' all this money outta their coat pockets and seams a their coats and jist paid for the whole place right there on the spot!

SALLY: No!

HESTER: It's the Lord's truth! See, Billy was jist hangin' aroun' that ole law office an Hawkins came out an told him the whole thing—an then Billy ran on down the road and caught up to 'em and TALKED to 'em!

SALLY: Oh, *pshaw!* What'd they say?

HESTER: Nothin' much Billy could understand—jist talkin' all this foreign jibberty-jaw! But ole man Hawkins tole Billy they come off a boat from Europe. Landed in Texas on the Gulf, then moved on up from New Orleans.

SALLY: Oh my stars! LIVE JEWS?!? What'd they look like? Billy say?

HESTER: Didn't say too much. Funny lookin', though, he did say that. Not nothin' like white folks, now that's a fact, he said.

SALLY: Crime'n It'ly! I can't hardly believe it—JEWS!!

HESTER: They're sellin' apples out in front a the place Billy said. Got a wagon full of 'em parked on the road. Windfall.

SALLY: Windfall?

HESTER: Ummm—See, their men folks took this wagon and went on out to the country—Dabny's farm—and jist went right onto his land an picked the windfall apples outta his orchard, from the ground. And then went on and done the same thing at the Johnson place. And now they're sellin' 'em off, Billy says. Right now. Today.

SALLY: Sunday?

HESTER: Well they're heathens, Sally Sue. Shoot, girl! Don't you know nothin'? It don't mean nothin' to them workin' on the Lord's Day—Hey—you got any money?

SALLY: Jist my donation is all.

HESTER: Well, I got six cents. Wonder how many a them windfall apples that'd buy?

SALLY: I don't know an I don't care! I got to go—

[SALLY *starts off, and* HESTER *comes after her.*]

HESTER: Aw, come on—walk on over there with me—it'd jist take ten minutes—an we could sneak on into church—back row. Nobody'll see us or nothin'—Sally Sue? Come on—let's go see!

[HESTER *stands in front of* SALLY, *taking her hand.*]

SALLY: No! I'd jist be too scairt, Hester! Now let me pass?

[SALLY *pushes by* HESTER, *who trails* SALLY *again.*]

HESTER: Don't have to be scairt. We don't have to go inside or nothin'. Billy says the apple cart is down by the road. We could jist watch across that road. We don't even have to say nothin' or buy nothin' if we don't want to—jist pass on by and stop an take a look . . . [HESTER *blocks* SALLY *again, who pushes her aside again.*] . . . and then we'll come right on back to church! Come on?

SALLY: I don't think so, Hester. I got to go to Sunday school, and I just know I'd be too scairt.

[HESTER *flounces away from* SALLY *in other direction.*]

HESTER: Well then, I'm goin' on by myself—an you ain't never gonna git no chance to see any live Jews or nothin' ever again—not with me, you ain't! An I'm gonna tell Bill what an old sissy scarety-cat you are.

[SALLY *starts off in the other direction.* HESTER *turns back.*]

Oh my! I did remember one other thing Billy had said—

SALLY: What?

HESTER: [*Giggling.*] The Jew men got theirselves horns on their heads!

[SALLY *laughs, too.*] And know what else?

SALLY: [*Giggling still.*] What?

HESTER: They wears hats all day long and never takes 'em off—jist to hide them horns!

[*They both are in fits of laughter now.*]

SALLY: No! I swear I never heard a such a thing in my life!

HESTER: Know what else?

SALLY: What?

HESTER: They got tails!

SALLY: TAILS?? Oh, Lord—TAILS?

HESTER: [*Convulsed in laughter.*] Bill—Billy says—they—they wears—long coats—to cover 'em up!

SALLY: [*Starts laughing, too.*] Land a Goshen, Hester! Oh my Land!

HESTER: Hey—come on—come on an go? You know you're jist dyin' to see it all. You jist know you are! COME ON!!

[HESTER *takes* SALLY*'s hand, pulling her.*]

SALLY: Oh Hester—I shouldn't—I jist shouldn't go at all—[SALLY *lets herself be pulled along.*]

We can't stay long though—we got to git right back fast, hear?? Promise me that.

[HESTER *and* SALLY *are exiting the stage.*]

HESTER: Sure, sure—now hurry up and come on—Oooeee!!

[*As lights fade we hear the girls singing as they run along the country road.* HESTER *and* SALLY *are singing a country folksong from long ago:*]

HESTER and SALLY: "Oh WE belong to Uncle Sam,

Sing-song Kitsy Kitsy Kai-me-o.

Oh, WE belong to Uncle Sam,

Sing-song Kitsy Kitsy Kai-me-oh.

Kay-mo, Kai-mo, Uncle Sam,

M'hey, M'hi, M'hum-drum

Go away, THEY go way THEY GO WAY:

Uruguay! Paraguay!

Oh! WE belong to Uncle Sam!

Sing-song Kitsy Kitsy Kai-me-oh!"

[*Singing,* HESTER and SALLY *come to another part of the road. A wagon with apples is on one side, bushes are on other.* HESTER *and* SALLY*'s voices die out as they spy an apple wagon and hide behind the bush on other side of the road, peeking out, whispering.*]

HESTER: Now, all we gotta do is wait—be quiet, an wait—

SALLY: [*Whispering too, but losing courage.*] I jist feel so funny, though, Hester. Truly I do. I don't know what it's gonna be like seein' no Jews! But it sure feels evil! It bein' Sunday an all—it jist feels EVIL! Oh Hester, I don't—

[SARAH *enters, carrying a crudely handwritten sign that reads "APPLES 5 cents". She sticks the sign on her wagon and rearranges the apples.* SALLY *and* HESTER *start whispering again:*]

SALLY: Oh Land! Look at her with that ole funny scarf an all—an she's so dark! She looks evil, Hester! Jist so EVIL!

HESTER: Hey—know what they say?

SALLY: What?

HESTER: All their women opens up sideways down there—

SALLY: What?

HESTER: Chink women does, too—slanty like their eyes—jist like a cat.

SALLY: Stop that! Don't go talkin' filthy dirty like that on the Lord's Day. Please Hester? Don't? We're gonna git punished for sure! Lightenin' or thunder's gonna strike us—or tornadoes or—

HESTER: Hush up, scarety-cat! Ain't nothin' gonna happen to us.

SALLY: Well don't you talk dirty like that again!

HESTER: [*Giggling.*] Ain't dirty—it's a fact a life!

[SARAH *exits.*]

Hey—know what else is a fact a life?

SALLY: No! An I don't wanna! I jist want outta here!

HESTER: Their men is in two parts down there—

SALLY: Huh?

HESTER: They cut 'em in half down there when they's babies. They got two dinghies!

[HESTER *smothers her laughter.*]

SALLY: An they livin' HERE? PLEASE—LET'S GO?

[*Grabs* HESTER's *hand, tries pulling her away.*]

HESTER: Let go! I wanna see her some more—besides she's jist a girl. She can't hurt us—but you better not bring your brother round here, 'cause they kill other people's baby boys. Now that's a fact a—

[SARAH *reappears carrying a stack of baskets for her apples. She hears, sees* SALLY *and* HESTER.]

SARAH: [*Hesitantly, with accent, speaks memorized words she doesn't understand.*] Hello—Hello—how—are—you—?

[SARAH *starts to cross the road to where* HESTER *and* SALLY *are, trying to see them behind the bush, shading her eyes. Now she points back to the wagon. Understands these words:*]

Apples? Five cents?—*Du vielst?* [*Translation: Do you want?*]

SALLY: [*Terrified.*] Law! She's puttin' some kinda curse on us, Hester! Oh Law!

[HESTER *takes on this dare and steps out into road.*]

HESTER: Don't you come no step closer to us! We don't want nothin' off you! We don't want no stolen apples, hear?

SARAH: [*Not comprehending.*] "Stol-en"? *Ich forshtayin zee nisht!* [*Translation: I don't understand you.*]

SALLY: OOHH!! She cursed AGAIN! Oh my stars—let's run! She's a WITCH!!

HESTER: [*Not intimidated.*] I told you we don't want no stolen apples off you! An you keep off a us! This here's a state public road an we got our rights, hear? Or I'll git my pa after you! You got no business here, anyhow. You don't really live here—an them's stolen goods!

SARAH: [*Smiling, holding out basket, saying her memorized words.*] Hel-lo—how—are—you?

[*Her smile fades. Something is very wrong.*]

SARAH: *Vos iss de mer—vos iss de mer mitt ourns?* [*Translation: What is the matter—what is the matter with you?*]

[*At this burst of Yiddish,* HESTER *grabs a stone and hurls it, hitting* SARAH *on her arm. Baskets fall to the ground as* SARAH *cries out in pain.* SALLY *breaks away, running, screaming:*]

SALLY: WITCH!! WITCH!!

HESTER: Now you keep away from us! Don't you dare put no curse on us. JIST KEEP AWAY—KEEP AWAY!!

[HESTER *is backing up, holding* SARAH *at bay, then* HESTER *runs off.* SARAH *is sobbing, holding her arm. A beat.*]

SARAH: [*Screaming after them, hateful and patronizingly:*] SHIKSAS!! SHIKSAS!! [*Translation: Gentile girls! Gentile girls!*]

[*A moment. Then* SARAH *picks up the pile of baskets, goes to her wagon, and stacks the baskets. Then she determinedly takes her sign and sticks it in a row of apples so it's more visible. She looks in the direction of the girls then yanks the babushka from her head, gathers her dark hair to the nape of her neck, twists the babushka into a long cord-like scarf, and ties it at nape of neck as girls wear their hair. She looks down road the other way for next customers. With much bravado, she begins reciting, doing it better with each recitation:]*

SARAH: "Hel-lo? How—are—you? Apples—five—cents. Hello! How are you—apples—

[*As* SARAH *speaks, we hear* SALLY *and* HESTER *sing as they run along the country road to church:*]

"Oh, WE belong to Uncle Sam,

Sing-song Kitsy Kitsy Kai-me-oh!

WE belong to Uncle Sam—"

[*Their voices fade as lights fade.*]

END OF PLAY

YOUTH DANCE

Wayne Paul Mattingly

Youth Dance was originally produced in 2009 by Karen's After Dark, in Brewster, New York. It was directed by the author, and had the following cast:

GISELLE: Quinn Warren
TOMMY: Michael Pinnachio

CHARACTERS

TOMMY: *14 years old. He is dressed in a suit and tie that are too large for him. He wears a corsage in his lapel.*

GISELLE: *14 years old. She is dressed in a pastel pink or light blue floral party dress and wears a wrist corsage.*

TIME

Although both characters seem as though they are from the 1950s, it is actually the present day.

SETTING

A small town in rural New England. A school dance. Evening. GISELLE, *a fourteen-year-old wheelchair-bound romantic, has come to the school dance as classmate* TOMMY's *date.* TOMMY, *prompted by friends to find out* GISELLE's *sexual "condition," experiences the eruption of conflicting feelings of violence and attraction before he discovers in* GISELLE *a friend who allows him to reveal his family anguish, and to possibly discover with her a teen romance*

> "The energy of the stars becomes us,
> and we become the energy of the stars."
> ~*Dennis Kucinich*

GISELLE, *in her wheelchair, is in a remote garden with sculpture outside a school building from which the music of a social dance is heard. She is looking up at the sky.* TOMMY *joins her.*

TOMMY: Sorry . . . I didn't see you—

GISELLE: No, it's—

TOMMY: —had gone.

GISELLE: —okay. It's pretty out tonight.

TOMMY: . . . outside. Yeah, it's . . .

GISELLE: [*She looks up at him.*] Pretty.

TOMMY: Yeah. [*Pause.*] Sorry.

GISELLE: It's all right, really.

TOMMY: Yeah, but, I don't know . . . you're my date.

GISELLE: I'm happy to be here, Tommy. If you hadn't asked me, I'd be home watching tonight's *Classic Movie*. Or reruns of *The Simpsons*.

TOMMY: Do you like that show?

GISELLE: Which one?

TOMMY: *Classic Movie.*

GISELLE: I love the old black-and-white films, where everyone's dashing around in evening gowns and tuxedos. They look like . . .

TOMMY: They wanted me . . .

GISELLE: . . . What?

TOMMY: Sorry.

GISELLE: No, what?

TOMMY: They wanted me to find out . . .

GISELLE: Who? Eddie?

TOMMY: Yeah, and Ashley . . .

GISELLE: Oh.

TOMMY: . . . and, you know, Zack and Molly. Tell them . . .

GISELLE: Huh. Wait. Find out what?

TOMMY: Um, what you . . . you know, you were . . . like.

GISELLE: [*A comment to herself:*] Huh.

TOMMY: Felt like.

GISELLE: Felt like? You mean, like rubber or wood? My legs, or what?

TOMMY: Don't get mad. I didn't tell them.

GISELLE: Oh, please. This is not mad, Tommy, this—

TOMMY: I couldn't tell them, really . . .

GISELLE: . . . is far from—No, you couldn't.

> [*Long uncomfortable pause.* TOMMY *goes to* GISELLE's *wheelchair and spins it around towards him. He kisses her. She lifts up her arms and embraces him and they kiss a long sweet teenage kiss. He places his hands on her legs, then under them.*]

GISELLE: [*Snaps chair locks on, then, softly.*] What are you doing?

[*He begins to lift her.*]

TOMMY: You'll see.

[*He lifts her up, holds her in the air a moment, swaying.*]

GISELLE: Are we dancing?

TOMMY: Yeah.

GISELLE: I follow well, don't I?

TOMMY: You feel so . . . alive in my arms. Your body moves . . .

GISELLE: But my legs, my legs are like, like what, Tommy?

TOMMY: Soft. Soft stillness.

[*Pleased with himself.*]

GISELLE: A still life.

TOMMY: No! Like a Rubens, a painting . . . that *captures* life . . . without *being* life!

GISELLE: You're sweet.

TOMMY: I take art class.

GISELLE: I see.

TOMMY: And I feel your rib cage swell and fall with each breath and . . . there's movement in your hips, even though you're in my arms like this I can feel your hips sway, a pendulum . . .

GISELLE: Let's go. Take me for a ride. [TOMMY *swings* GISELLE *around and seats her in her chair. He walks behind her and kisses her neck. Pause.*] Tommy? [*He doesn't answer.*] Tommy? Are you . . . ? [*She tries to turn around, but he wheels her forward recklessly fast.*] Tommy! Stop! [*She screams. He abruptly pulls to stop, throwing* GISELLE *from chair.*]

TOMMY: Ohmygod! Ohmygod!

GISELLE: Whoa! God!

TOMMY: I'M SORRY, I'M SO SORRY, GISELLE! GISELLE!

GISELLE: My dress. I'm okay, I'm okay. [*Pause.*] Help me up.

[*Instead, he sits next to her.*]

TOMMY: Giselle?

GISELLE: What are you going to tell them, Tom?

TOMMY: Hmm? Who? Oh, them. About? Oh!

GISELLE: What did they want to know?

TOMMY: Oh, god, you know, what I told you.

GISELLE: And?

TOMMY: Nothing.

GISELLE: And will you tell them my legs are like a Rubens? Or like sausages?

TOMMY: Heaven. Like heaven in my hands, in my arms . . .

GISELLE: Heaven? Ho! My legs are *in* heaven, I hope. Have you ever heard that song where the guy in it loses an arm and it's reattached in heaven?

TOMMY: No.

GISELLE: I'd like that. To know the life in my legs would be rejoined one day.

TOMMY: They wanted to know, for me to find out . . .

GISELLE: Yes?

TOMMY: [*Rising.*] If, you know . . .

GISELLE: Nope. I sure don't. Help me up now.

[TOMMY *climbs up and sits on the adjacent "sculpture." Pause.*]

TOMMY: They wanted to know if you were, you know . . . uh, lame, lifeless . . . down there.

GISELLE: Lame? *Down there?*

TOMMY: I don't know. I know it sounds stupid.

GISELLE: I'm not lame!

TOMMY: I don't know! I . . .

GISELLE: I'm fourteen!

TOMMY: I know, I—I—

GISELLE: Tommy. We've gone out, what? Never? To a movie not really a date, and, and . . .

[*He jumps down almost too close to* GISELLE.]

TOMMY: I was . . . I was . . . [*He changes direction, locks down the wheelchair.*] . . . curious. They just asked me what your legs felt like. Holding you, touching you, I, I just wanted to know how you felt . . . maybe, you were like. [*He picks her up, sits in the wheelchair with* GISELLE *on his lap.*] I wanted you. [*They exchange smiles, grins.*] Want. To know.

[*She unbuttons her dress, takes his hand from her lap and puts it on her breast.*]

GISELLE: I'm fourteen.

TOMMY: So am I. It's so warm and soft.

GISELLE: Do you like it?

TOMMY: Oh, yes. Oh! Your nipple! It's . . .

GISELLE: Alert.

TOMMY: Yeah, I'll say.

GISELLE: Why were you crying before?

[*He withdraws his hand from her breast. She begins to button up.*]

TOMMY: When?

GISELLE: Before, when you were kissing my neck.

TOMMY: Huh?

GISELLE: I felt your tears on my neck.

TOMMY: I was . . . I was . . .

GISELLE: Yes?

TOMMY: . . . my mom. My mom . . . she's drunk again. She called before. She's too drunk to pick us up. I . . .

GISELLE: I'm sorry.

TOMMY: I was trying to get a ride home for us with Eddie or Zack—They know my mom. They know she can do this, they've seen it firsthand.

GISELLE: She seemed all right earlier.

TOMMY: She gets . . . loaded, little by little, as soon as she gets home from work, she just keeps drinking, sipping wine, mostly, but continuously, and I, I didn't want you . . .

GISELLE: It's okay, it's okay.

TOMMY: I like you so much, Giselle—and look how clear and beautiful the night sky is! It's warm and cool with gentle breezes that tickle—but it's not cold—and the stars are flickering and shimmering and, and you're here, you're here in my arms, on my lap, warm and, and full of, of soft stillness . . .

[*She leans back to kiss him. They look up at the sky.*]

GISELLE: It's a glorious night. All those wishes in the heavens! For us. For us, Tommy!

TOMMY: [*Breaking down as he goes on.*] She'll be passed out somewhere—in the living room, hanging over the sofa or splayed out on her bed like, like, I don't wanna say, half dressed and some half-empty booze bottle nearby—she's very unhappy, so very unhappy, I know, but sometimes . . .

GISELLE: [*Tender.*] I know, I know . . .

TOMMY: . . . sometimes—I have homework and, and, I just want to take her and shake her bones right out of her body and I don't want to go home and see that, see her, I can't . . .

GISELLE: Tommy, it's only two miles . . .

TOMMY: . . . I can't be there.

GISELLE: . . . to my house from here! Two miles! Drive me home!

TOMMY: I can't! Drive!? I don't have a car or . . .

GISELLE: Me! Me! Drive me in my wheelchair home!

TOMMY: Really? Yeah?

GISELLE: Drive *in* the chair! *With* me!

TOMMY: All the way?

GISELLE: Part way. Some. You can push me the rest.

TOMMY: Yeah? Okay. Okay!

[*He begins to play with the wheelchair.*]

GISELLE: And maybe, maybe you can sleep over at my house.

We'll spend our first night together, and in the morning my mother will make us breakfast and, and you can brush out my hair, and we can drink coffee and eat toast like they do in the movies. Let's go, let's go, Tommy! My parents will love that you've "driven" me home on such a splendid night. Look at that moon! It's so brilliant. Like a secret passageway to another way of being. Let's go! [TOMMY *begins to "drive" her off.*] We could be falling in love, you know.

TOMMY: How would we know?

GISELLE: Maybe we wouldn't. We wouldn't know until we got there. It feels like *something* now, though, doesn't it?

TOMMY: Yeah, it does feel like . . . falling, or like when you jump off a diving board, you're in midair . . .

GISELLE: Is *that* what it feels like? This?

TOMMY: Yeah, yeah it does, up in midair with no gravity and a sudden plunging . . .

GISELLE: Into another world.

TOMMY: Water.

GISELLE: Like birth, being born, in reverse.

TOMMY: What?

GISELLE: Nothing. Something girls think about as soon as we're able.

TOMMY: I'd like to fall in love with you, Giselle.

GISELLE: Me, too. I mean fall in love with you.

TOMMY: [*As they exit.*] I knew you meant that. I mean me.

GISELLE: Well, yeah. Not fall in love with myself. Duh. [*Slight pause.*] I feel that, Tommy.

END OF PLAY